"Oh my goodness, I was right there, riding with you in my mind. What a wonderful gift you have. Your memories become so clear in my mind's eye that I could actually feel the wind in my hair and my adrenaline pumping on the ride up the mountain. Thank you for bringing me back to that simple time, I have missed it!"
~ Kim Devitte

"'Bumblebees and Dandelions' is your best story yet. I just realized I say that about all of them. You truly paint magical pictures of a little boy's mind. You make me read in color. Thank you for this gift. Keep them coming."
~ Rose Bruno

"I love your stories. You take me back to special times in my life like no one else ever has! I'm right there. I see what you're seeing, hear what you're hearing, living this story with you. Thank you once again for sharing these precious memories!"
~ Vandy Winker Palazzo

"When I was in high school, Bob taught me how to play chess in the cafeteria. Bob was a storyteller even back then, so it is no surprise that I'm laughing today about bingo daubers and chess. His love story 'Destiny' will warm your heart and inspire you to take chances – to zig when you feel like zagging. His friends have enjoyed these stories for years, and now you can too. They make us smile, giggle and rekindle memories of days gone by. They remind us time and again of what true love looks like in every form, and they make us feel like we are on top of the world."
~ Angela Vicino Mecca

"Your story about your mom was so sweet that it made me cry. Thanks again for sharing."
~ Patricia Evans

"What a touching story! I can remember collecting dandelion 'flowers' for my mom!"
~ Diane Spendio Cimino

"Heartwarming story about bumblebees and dandelions. Enjoyed every word."
~ Linda Henry Hayes

"Great story! I am amazed at your memory! Loved the part in 'It's Academic' where you went home and had lunch with your mother. Our mother was home for us too. I would give anything to be able to do that again."
~ Anna Bongiovanni

"You had me laughing at the description of the cloak room. Thank you, Bob!"
~ Laura Mendola

"You had me at Robert P. Simpson!"
~ Kathy Wade Iodice

"It's always wonderful to hear a man speak so sweetly of his wife, as this author does in 'Destiny'. That's special. But I hate that the stories have an ending. I could read on forever."
~ Toni Manzare

"You have such a knack for relating all the feelings I'm sure we all felt as young Catholics! You should write a book!"
~ Patricia L. Edukonis

"I remember those days in church. You brought back so many memories. Wow! I love your stories. Keep them coming!"
~ Marie Leo Lorenzoni

"Mr. Simpson, the story about your epic bike ride touched me. Thank you for the adventure. I look forward to these memories you share with us."
~ Terry Tompkins

"Well, you did it again! But this time I am in tears! Loved hearing this story about you and your friends coming of age on your bicycles."
~ Joni Bonaro Fernandez

"I think the bicycling story is my favorite so far. (Then again each time you write one it becomes my favorite so far.) You truly have a gift. I can see your stories playing out in my mind as vividly as if I'm watching a movie."
~ Jennifer Romanek Santora

"If that Dahlia Bulb story is HALF TRUE, I will kiss you on both cheeks DUE BACI!"
~ William F. Savino, Esq.

"'Top of the World' really touched my heart. I love reading your stories!"
~ Maureen Mahoney-Vitello

"'Top of the World' is the best one yet. Tears in my eyes for your friend."
~ Marie Giordano Campagna

"OMG, Dahlia Bulbs is hilarious! Love those Italian names!"
~ Rena Ponzi Previte

"LMAO about your Dahlia Bulbs. Yes, in Niagara Falls you were Italian or you were nobody. LOL."
~ Penny Ferro Arbulu

"What a beautifully written account about newspaper carriers. Thank you Robert P. Simpson for warming my heart and brightening my day with these great memories of my much-loved paper route."
~ Lisa Castiglione Wheaton

"Just started reading your stories, and I'm loving them. Keep them coming, please."
~ Ursula Strong

"I loved 'Spelling Baseball'. I could envision the classroom with the girls in their dresses on one side and the boys on the other neatly dressed. The kids standing tall against the chalkboards and bulletin boards. You bring back such fun memories from back in simpler times in our lives."
~ Kerrie Keller Piaskowski

"I just knew my favorite Bob-Tale, 'Destiny', would find its way to print! Perhaps this beautiful love story will give a reader renewed hope in finding love or even make them believe in destiny!"
~ Kathy Dembek

"'Destiny' — Now THAT is one great story."
~ Barbara Roman

"Lovely memories once again. Sometimes it is the simple things we remember that brought joy to our hearts."
~ Lynn Field Draper

"I left Niagara Falls in 1974. Every one of your stories is so vivid that I feel like I'm my young self back home again. Love the memories!"
~ Lorraine Zito

"What a wonderful memory for me! I was thrilled when I was not chosen for the *It's Academic* team, and always

believed that you, Stephanie and Mike were our best chance to win. Even without the victory it was a great day. Thanks for an excellent story!"
~ Loralee Wilson Hamel
(NFHS *It's Academic* team 1974)

"You did it again! I love the story about punctuation and emoticons! You, friend, are the gift that keeps on giving! Looking forward to reading your next creation!"
~ Cherie Visciano-Fineberg

"As a former librarian, I can't help but love this piece about punctuation and emoticons. It may be my favorite."
~ Gayle Miller Kerman

"LOL – the 'cloakroom'! Don't you just hate how publishers now have only one space between sentences? I myself still type two spaces between sentences; I think everyone should be doing that. You wrote another great story!"
~ Lynne Kukulka Ficorilli

"'Christmas, Carrots, and a Cat Named Charlie' is one of my favorite stories. It brought back many childhood Christmas memories."
~ Joy LeBrasseur Evans

Bumblebees & Dandelions

Tales to Make You Laugh, Smile, and Remember

By Robert P. Simpson

Illustrations by Frank A. Mariani

LIBRASTREAM
BUFFALO, NEW YORK

Copyright © 2019 by Robert P. Simpson

Foreword Copyright © 2019 by Sandy Fabiano Supon

"Mining for Gold on Niagara Avenue" Copyright © 2019 by Michael J. Simpson

EDGE® is a registered trademark of Edgewell Personal Care Brands, LLC

All rights reserved. No part of this book may be reproduced or transmitted in any form by any means, electronic or mechanical, including photocopying and recording, or by any information storage or retrieval system, except as may be expressly permitted by the 1976 Copyright Act or in writing from the publisher.

www.bumblebeesanddandelions.com

Rights and Permissions: john@librastream.com

Publisher: John R. Randolph

Cover Art and Illustrations: Frank A. Mariani

Designer: Leslie Taylor
Buffalo Creative Group,
www.buffalocreativegroup.com

Editor: Sallie G. Randolph

Copy Editor: Adelina Simpson

Publisher's Cataloging-in-Publication Data

Names:	Simpson, Robert P., author. | Mariani, Frank A., illustrator.
Title:	Bumblebees and dandelions : tales to make you laugh, smile, and remember / by Robert P. Simpson ; illustrations by Frank A. Mariani.
Description:	Buffalo, New York : Librastream, [2019]
Identifiers:	ISBN: 9781680610123 (hardcover) | 9781680610130 (paperback) | 9781680610338 (library edition) | 9781680610147 (ebook) | 9781680610321 (audiobook) | LCCN: 2019941755
Subjects:	LCSH: Coming of age--New York (State)--Niagara Falls. | Storytellers--Biography. | Nostalgia. | Children. | Adulthood. | Middle age. | Love. | Family. | Friendship. | Humorous stories, American. | Short stories, American. | LCGFT: Humor. | Short stories. | BISAC: BIOGRAPHY & AUTOBIOGRAPHY / Personal Memoirs. | HUMOR / Topic / Cultural, Ethnic & Regional.
Classification:	LCC: PS3619.I56395 B86 2019 | DDC: 813.6--dc23

LIBRASTREAM
BUFFALO, NEW YORK

Printed in the United States of America

Dedication

This work is dedicated to my wife, Ellen, who endured many of these stories for years before she playfully suggested that I start sharing them with others. I wrote "Destiny" for her. This work is also dedicated to my daughter, Adelina, the creative writer in the family. The title story, "Bumblebees and Dandelions", is written in memory of my late sister, Kathleen Ann, born with spina bifada, and dedicated to my mom and dad in Heaven, where they are all now laughing together. "Top of the World" is dedicated to my dear friend, the late Dan Mitulinksy.

Table of Contents

Acknowledgements

Foreword

Preface

Bumblebees and Dandelions 1

Christmas, Carrots, and a
   Cat Named Charlie 8

Exploding Angel Food Cake 16

Lost in Niagara Falls 21

Spelling Baseball 30

Holy Thursday and Ringing the Bells 36

The Big Pool 48

Sting-Ray Bicycles and
   José Feliciano Burglar Alarms 55

Delivering the News 61

The Day my Coach Listened to Me 70

The Music Man at Gaskill Junior High....................... 77

Dating in the 70s — the Seven-digit
    Stutter Step 85

The Race.. 89

A Teacher for the Ages and His Factual Sh!ts............. 99

It's Academic 105

What are Clouds Made Of?.. 115

Fast Food Cashiers and Microphones 124

Is He Rehabilitatable? 130

Destiny 136

Dahlia Bulbs and Sauce 142

Wine Tastings and the
    Law School Admission Test 145

Marriage and the Lottery... 152

Store Returns.. 155

Bingo or Chess? 159

Tax Law, True Love,
    and the Socratic Method 165

A Day at Niagara with a Phony Tour Guide 172

Men's Cologne and a
    Hug from My Pharmacist 177

My "itis" 181

Wagging Tails and Hearts of Gold 185

Shaving Cream in the
    Passenger Compartment 191

Punctuation and Emoticons 196

Top of the World.. 203

A Kid Brother's Tale
    Mining for Gold on Niagara Avenue
    by Michael J. Simpson.. 219

About the Author

Acknowledgements

I never set out to write this book, only to tell some stories, and it never would have happened but for my awesome wife, Ellen, playfully suggesting that I start telling my stories to others. Thank you, sweetheart, for encouraging me at every step to see this project through to the end, and for picking up the slack in our law practice as I did so. Most of my stories are love stories, and you are the love of my life.

Writing a book is harder than I ever imagined, and I want to thank my friend and colleague in the law, Sallie Randolph, for serving as my writing coach and editor. Sallie and I spent countless hours together on weekends critiquing each story, each paragraph, each sentence, and each word. Every writer, especially a first-time author, should have someone like Sallie as a coach.

Sallie's husband, John, my publisher, guided me through the process. I was glad to rely on John for an honest, objective opinion about what worked and what didn't. Thank you John and Librastream for taking a chance on my book.

Writing and editing are two different skill sets, and I am grateful to my daughter, Adelina, for her excellent work in copy editing this book. As a law student, Adelina served as Executive Publications Editor for the Buffalo Law Review, and I soon learned why she was elected to that prestigious position. Thank you, sweetheart, for your good work on my book, and for teaching me the difference between an "en" dash and an "em" dash!

There was never a doubt as to whom I would turn to illustrate my stories. My dear friend Frank Mariani is an amazing artist. We've done patent drawings and law firm advertisements together for years, and I have always been in awe of his talent. Frank has a special gift of listening to an idea or reading a few words of my text and then drawing exactly what was heretofore only in my mind's eye. He makes my stories come alive as only he could. Thank you, Frank!

My thanks, also, to Leslie Taylor of Buffalo Creative Group for her excellent work on the design. As a first-time author I didn't even know we needed a book designer, or even what one did! It soon became clear that Leslie was the hub in the center who coordinated and pulled together all the parts of the book. Thank you, Leslie!

Thank you to Edgewell Personal Care Brands, LLC for permission to use both the famous EDGE® registered trademark and the image of the EDGE® shaving gel can in my story. This is the only shaving gel I have ever used.

It was a sad day when I lost some of this great product in the passenger compartment of my car.

I want to thank my many friends who took the time to read these stories and send me "likes," "ha-has," "hearts," and comments. It was their encouragement and kind words that inspired me to write more. There are too many to mention by name, but I especially want to thank Anna and Rosa, Larry and Gayle, Toni-Jean, Mary and Kathy, Laura, Penny, Theresa, Mary Ann, Jessica, Baby Mary, Joyce, Maureen, Vic and Joan, Ernie, Fran, Colleen, Gail, Cindy, Lynn, Lynne, Rena, Donna, Jenn, Jade, Joy, Kerrie, Cherie, Rose, Michelle and Marcia, Toni, Barb, Pam, Karen, Amy, Denise, Diane and Margot.

Finally, there are four special friends I want to acknowledge and thank. Writing is personal, and sometimes a writer needs a sounding board and private review before going public. Sandy Fabiano Supon and Angela Vicino Mecca, friends since our school days, reviewed many of my stories before I showed them to anyone else. Our friendships extend over decades and I trusted these dear friends to tell me the truth, good or bad, before anyone else saw my stories. Kathy Dembek, also a dear friend since junior high, has sent me countless messages of encouragement along this journey. We share a common goal of wanting to help those afflicted with spina bifada, and I hope we can make a difference. Writing has also brought me a special new friend, Marcia

Brown Eugeni. A writer sometimes never knows if his words make a difference, inspire a smile, a chuckle, or even a tear. Marcia let me know when I needed it most. Thank you, Marcia!

And then it happened...

Foreword

When I look back in life, there are so many moments that stand out. We all have them, but I believe that those times in school and the friendships made and shared there were especially meaningful.

I have known the author, Robert P. Simpson, since junior high school and, although he will always be "Bob" to me, I always knew he was destined to do great things. He is a devoted husband to Ellen, the love of his life, and loving father to Adelina. He is a great lawyer, mediocre chess player, lousy bingo player, delightful writer, and dear friend.

This book of short stories that I lovingly call "Bob-Tales" magically takes you back to a time of fond memories and everlasting friendships. Bob has a way of painting pictures in your mind's eye with his words. You see what he sees in color as he describes these simpler times.

Some of these tales may bring a tear or two but mostly they will make you smile, sometimes chuckle, or even laugh out loud. I eagerly awaited each tale in this collection to appear. They have brought a welcome escape from life's troubles and cares, if but for a moment.

From grade school to middle age, and everywhere in-between, Bob's unique way of storytelling will undoubtedly stir memories of your own.

A big thank you to Ellen for her patience, sense of humor, and for encouraging Bob to share these stories with all of us. Thank you, Bob, for all your creative work in taking us back to those special places in time. This has been an incredible journey for you and for us. I am honored to have been a small part of it and honored to call you my friend.

Bob includes a trademark phrase in many of his stories: "And then it happened… ." As for you, dear reader, as you read each story and lament that it has ended, and look forward to the next, and as you relate these stories to events in your own life, remember what Dr. Seuss once said: "Don't cry because it's over. Smile because it happened."

Sandy Fabiano Supon
Youngstown, New York
July, 2019

Preface

I have always wondered why we are here and what we should do about it. We may never know, but while I'm here, I've decided to try and make people smile with strings of words that pop into my brain, trickle down to my fingertips and arrange themselves on a page. Most of these stories are true; the rest are mostly true. Some recall events from childhood, others more recent. My friends call them "Bob-Tales" and I'm fine with that. I'm just happy they read them. I hope you enjoy the stories. I hope they make you smile, laugh, and remember.

> Robert P. Simpson
> Williamsville, New York
> July, 2019

Bumblebees and Dandelions

When I was three years old, I spent a lot of time in my front yard and on the sidewalk in front of my house figuring things out. For example, I figured out that all the TVs in the United States came from Menkenna's TV Repair Shop across the street from my house. I knew this because I saw car after car pull up in front of the TV shop and person after person come out of the store carrying a TV.

I studied all sorts of stuff. I noticed that there were cracks in our sidewalk every couple of feet. I watched ants and other bugs crawl down into those cracks and never come out. I decided early on that I didn't want that to happen to me, so, to this day, I always try to avoid stepping on cracks in sidewalks. A lot of my friends do this too.

Every adult I met back then asked me the same two questions, in the same order: "What's your name?" and "How old are you?"

Day after day, my answer was the same: "My name is Robert and I'm three years old."

Adults always seemed surprised when a kid just blurted out his age instead of holding up fingers. A kid can have a lot of fun with that. By the time I was four, I had had enough. When some older mom or dad would ask me my age, I would tell them that I was 25 years old just to see their reaction.

I always wished people would ask me tougher questions when I was little, like: "How do televisions work?" or "What are you working on?"

I wished they would ask me about the big project I was working on in the spring and summer of my fourth year.

You see, when I was still three, I would follow my mom around the house all day long when my dad was at work. I would help her push the vacuum in the living room and the broom in the kitchen. I would stand on a stool and put the breakfast and lunch dishes in the sink. I would dry them after she washed them. Dusting the furniture was my favorite. We did that together every few days. My mom even let me spray the Lemon Pledge. When I showed Mom how well I could do these things she would smile.

One day she sat me down. "Close your eyes," she said.

I closed them and waited in anticipation. I could hear paper rustling and something jingling.

"OK, now you can look."

I opened my eyes to see a big blue piggy bank with a

slot on top and a cork in its belly. Next to the bank was a jar full of nickels and pennies.

"What's this, Mom?" I asked.

"The coins are your allowance," she explained. "You earn two cents for drying the lunch dishes, three cents for pushing the broom, and a nickel for polishing the furniture. The piggy bank is for saving all your coins."

I loved my mom. She asked me important questions like, "What do you want to be when you grow up?"

I had a good answer for that. I told her I wanted to be tall when I grew up. I told her, "I want to be tall enough to reach the cookies in the cupboard over the counter." It's tough always having to ask someone taller for a cookie, especially if it's your mom you are asking. Moms always keep track of how many cookies their kids eat in a day. Even today I think of my mom every time I reach for a cookie in a cupboard. I even think of her when I reach for sugar or spice.

I liked earning an allowance, but my favorite thing to do when I was little was to make my mom smile. I would do anything to make her smile. Mom seemed happiest of all when she was playing with me and my baby sister.

I don't remember too much about my sister, Kathleen Ann. She was born a few months after my third birthday. She was tiny and didn't walk or talk. Mom held her in her arms all the time. She sang to her, smiled at her, and made funny faces to make her laugh. She held her wrapped in a pink blanket all summer long. She carried her around the house as we did our chores together. She held Kathleen in her arms and me by the hand at the same time. She never let anyone else hold my sister, not even my dad. But she would let me make funny faces at her.

By the time the leaves changed colors on the trees in the fall of my third year, my mom stopped holding my sister in her arms. She stopped smiling and laughing too. I didn't know why. I didn't know where Heaven was or why Kathleen had gone there.

A few months later, on February 14, my dad came home from work with flowers for Mom. Flowers from a store! When Dad walked through the door with those flowers, I watched Mom smile at him. I had missed seeing that smile until then.

That's when I knew what I had to do. I had to find some flowers for her. I packed that thought away and held it in my brain and waited for the snow to melt. Every day for weeks and weeks I looked outside to see if the snow was gone. It took forever. It took two whole months.

Spring finally came, the sun came out, and flowers began popping up all around the neighborhood.

I launched my grand plan on a Saturday morning. I pulled my red Radio Flyer wagon onto our front lawn, and I picked every yellow flower I could find. I cleared the whole lawn.

Then I headed to our backyard and cleared that too.

I didn't know what kind of flowers they were, but they were bright yellow, and I just knew my mom would love them. I dropped to my knees to pick each one. I plucked each flower from the bottom of the stem and tossed them into my wagon.

When there wasn't a flower left to pick, I stuffed all the flowers into a big paper bag and carried the bag into the kitchen. I dumped the flowers onto the kitchen table. Then I pulled every drinking glass out of the cupboard, filled them all with water, and put the flowers into the glasses—just like my mom had done with her flowers from Dad. There must have been twenty glasses full of flowers on our kitchen table that day.

When I had them all arranged, I went and found Mom to show her my big surprise. "Close your eyes and come with me," I said, taking her hand and leading her into the kitchen. Dad tagged along behind us.

"OK, you can open them now," I said.

I could tell by my mom's smile that she loved them. Her eyes lit up and her smile almost turned into laughing because she loved them so much. My dad started to cough when he saw all the flowers. He coughed so hard that I thought he was going to cry. He was overcome by emotion.

Mom leaned over and told me in a soft voice that those were her most favorite flowers in the whole world. "They're dandelions," she said. They didn't look like lions to me, but if she loved them, that was good enough for me. There was such joy in our kitchen that day that I never wanted it to end.

We were especially lucky on Jerauld Avenue because we had thousands of the most beautiful flowers in the world on our street, and I set off with my wagon to pick every one. I could tell that all the moms and dads in our neighborhood were proud of me for bringing these flowers home to my mom. They let me have every flower on their front and back lawns. They all smiled when I had collected a wagonful. Mrs. Bax even gave me cookies and lemonade when I finished clearing her yard.

"Thank you, Robert," Mom said as she gave me a big hug with every batch.

It was hard work for a kid. You always had to wait until the bumblebees were done hovering over the flowers before you could pick them. By the time I had finished picking the flowers on half the street, I started to get worried. Mom had explained about the birds and the bees. I knew that birds slept in the trees and bees made honey from flowers.

I started to worry about the Jerauld Avenue honey supply. I'd better do something about that, I thought. So, I began collecting bumblebees. Those bees were fast, but I was faster. If you waited until they landed on a flower, and timed it just right, you could catch them in a jar.

When I had about twenty bumblebees in a jar, I took them home to Mom. I was just about to take the lid off the jar so the bees could make honey with the flowers in our kitchen when Mom stopped me. "I'll take care of that," she said, as she quickly took the jar from my hands. "Thank you for the bees."

I think she liked the flowers better than the bees.

I don't pick those flowers myself anymore. But every spring, when the dandelions pop up in our yard, I think about my mom. I think about how sweet she was, and how much she loved my baby sister, and how much she loved me.

Christmas, Carrots, and a Cat Named Charlie

There is nothing quite like the wonder and hope in a child's eyes on Christmas Eve. In the olden days, it may have been visions of sugar plums on the night before Christmas, but for me, it was visions of Lionel trains. I never tasted a sugar plum, but a Lionel American Flyer train with a whistle and a real, working chimney was something I could relate to. You could keep your sugar plums—I dreamt of a black locomotive pulling boxcars, flat cars, and a red caboose in a circle around my Christmas tree.

My two older sisters wasted their Christmas list ink on dolls. My list had a single, six-letter word, LIONEL, that I had painstakingly lettered in all capitals in Crayola red. I wanted to make it as easy as possible for Santa. He seemed to like red.

Back then, it wasn't easy for a kid to make his Christmas morning dreams come true. We had very few tools at our disposal—only the three "Bs" and the two "Ns."

We could Beg, Be good, and Behave. And we could be Naughty or Nice.

This was drilled into our heads with musical regularity. I learned early on that it's easy to be "naughty" but hard to spell it. It's easy to spell "nice" but harder to be, especially if you have two older sisters who always want to hug you and play dress-up.

It's not like you can just leave this being nice thing to chance, or just be nice when your mom and dad are watching you. There's this guy in a big red suit with a long white beard who isn't even your uncle and yet he knows all about you. He knows when you are sleeping. He knows when you're awake. And, worst of all, he knows if you've been bad or good.

This knowledge caused me no end of anxiety and sleepless nights. I checked over my shoulder all the time to see if he was watching. I checked under my bed for listening devices. I even examined my toys for hidden cameras. I had mixed emotions about this spying Santa Claus.

But Santa came through that year. I woke up Christmas morning at 5:00 a.m. sharp. Good thing, too, because everyone else had overslept.

"Merry Christmas," I shouted as I pranced from room to room. I know my mom and dad were grateful when I approached their bed. "Merry Christmas, Mom!" I repeated. "Merry Christmas, Dad!" Even my sisters got up right away without their usual grumbling.

There may have been other presents under the tree that year, but I don't remember any of them. All I saw was a brand-new Lionel O-Gauge train with a big black locomotive pulling six cars around our Christmas tree. The whistle was tooting, smoke was puffing from the chimney, and a headlight on the front of the locomotive lit up our living room on that Christmas morning.

I played with that Lionel train every single day until Easter, every single day until my older sister Mary accidentally dropped a metal fork across the tracks. Sparks flew, the transformer exploded, and tears filled my eyes. I never knew one kitchen fork could do so much damage. My train was gone and my heart was broken.

My dad explained "short circuit" to me in as kind a way as a father could. He even bought me a baseball mitt to help me get over this disaster.

By the time summer rolled around, I had mostly forgotten about that toy from my younger days. I was now old enough to dream big. I could count and I could read and I fully trusted this Santa fellow. He had come through with the train after all.

By the end of summer, I had finished reading the best book ever written, *The Black Stallion* by Walter Farley. It was a hard read for a kid my age, but it was a real page-turner. Mom helped me with the big words and sometimes she'd read a few chapters while I snuggled next to her on the couch.

By Halloween, I was starting to plan for Christmas. I could print quite neatly by now, so I borrowed some of Mom's note paper and stamps. I lettered my list and only had to erase twice.

I put my list in an envelope and pasted on six stamps, just to be sure it was enough. I used a clicker pen from Mom's desk to address the envelope. No point in taking any chances on a pencil smudge obscuring the address. "Santa Claus" I printed in ink. "North Pole." Then I took that letter to the corner mailbox. I stood on my tiptoes, stretched my arms as high as I could, and just managed to grasp the handle. I pulled back the door and tossed my envelope into the mailbox.

Now came the endless wait. And now it was time to concentrate on the three Bs and two Ns.

My friends that year were asking for ponies. Some of my "I believe in Santa" friends even asked for a Shetland pony. Not me. I wanted a horse—a full-grown horse. And not a Palomino, Morgan or Appaloosa, either. Oh no, I wanted a stallion—a big, tall, strong black stallion! If Santa came through, I planned to name him Walter after my favorite author.

Well, Santa didn't come through that year. There was no horse under our tree on Christmas morning, just an Eldon 1/32 scale slot car set that wasn't even on my list.

My dad tried his best to explain it to me. "Robert," he

said, "Santa could barely fit down the chimney himself with all the toys. There was just no way for him to come down riding a horse. Besides, horses are afraid of fire, so there is no way a stallion would follow Santa down."

I started to have serious doubts about old Santa. My pony-less friends in the neighborhood had their doubts too. We discussed the situation often during kindergarten recess. We whispered in argument during our nap times in Mrs. Brown's class about whether he was real or not.

"He's real!" Timmy insisted. It was easy for Timmy to believe. His father was a doctor and he got everything he asked for.

"He is not," said Ken, who never did get his Louisville Slugger baseball bat.

"I'm undecided," said Marvin.

I myself was skeptical. But I had a plan. I had math skills. I could add and subtract.

I didn't wait for Halloween that year. I embarked on my plan shortly after Labor Day. I made out my list. I inked out two words with an "or" in between them. I even drew pictures of a kitten and a puppy. I wasn't particular. Santa could decide. He would have four whole months to make a believer out of little Robert. I told no one about my list, not even my mom and dad.

That Christmas Eve in my sixth year, I put my plan into action. I poured a glass of milk and put it on the end table near the tree. I arranged three Christmas cookies on a plate next to the milk. But I was as skeptical as a kid without a black stallion could be. So, I went to the veg-

etable bin of the refrigerator, ripped open a bag of carrots, and carefully counted out eight carrots for those reindeer. Dasher, Dancer, Prancer, and friends would have a feast at my house. I never knew a reindeer that could pass up a carrot. Never mind that I never knew a reindeer either.

And then I did something I regretted for years—I counted the carrots still left in the bag, wrote the number on a sheet of paper, taped the paper to the fridge, and went to bed.

Visions of puppies and kittens, and carrots, danced in my head that night.

To my great surprise, my mom and dad and sisters were all up before I was that morning. I found them waiting by the tree along with my new baby brother. They must have been surprised when I walked right past them, stopped by the end table to see that the milk was half gone, the cookies were nibbled, and the carrots were missing.

I just had to know, so I ran to the kitchen, yanked open the fridge, and pulled open the vegetable bin.

I sank to the floor and counted the carrots in the bag. I counted them twice and checked the tally against the note I left on the fridge, and then I started to cry.

"What's wrong?" my mom asked, when I entered the living room in tears.

"There's twenty-two carrots in the bag!" I cried. She didn't seem to understand, and so I painfully explained the arithmetic.

"There were fourteen carrots in the bag on Christmas Eve. I wrote it down and checked it twice."

"So what?" asked my sister Gloria.

"Don't you see? There are no reindeer!" The logic of mathematics was irrefutable. I couldn't bring myself to tell them what else I had figured out, but I could tell they knew where I was headed.

"The reindeer probably ate their fill at the Miller's house," Dad said.

"Yes, and they weren't hungry when they got to our house," Mom added.

But I wasn't buying it.

And then it happened...

The sound came from the far side of the tree—faint at first.

"What is that sound?" Gloria asked. "It's getting louder."

"It sounds like a meow!" Mary said.

I was confused. I was perplexed. I looked at my mom and dad. I wiped the tears from my face with my pajama sleeve and strained to hear.

"I think it's coming from behind the tree," Dad said.

I bolted around the tree and there, peering timidly from under the lid of a Christmas-wrapped shoebox, was the cutest little black, white, and gray kitten you could ever hope for. A tag hung from his collar: "To Robert, from Santa." I immediately named him Charlie.

Well, the tears returned when I held Charlie in my arms that Christmas morning, but they were a different kind of tears. He became my new best friend. I sat on the floor in front of the couch watching my sisters open their presents. Charlie sat on the couch behind me and scratched an itch on the top of my head.

I scratched my head too, for years, about that Christmas morning.

I think about that morning every Christmas season. I also think about that morning whenever I eat carrots. I make it a point never to count the carrots on my plate, or in the refrigerator vegetable bin.

I don't need to count carrots. I'm a believer—in Christmas!

Exploding Angel Food Cake

We had a birthday tradition in our family. If it was your birthday, you got to pick the cake. I always loved this tradition. I think it is a sign of true love if you know someone's favorite birthday cake flavor. I also think it is true love if you know how someone takes their coffee.

On the day before my seventh birthday, Mom knelt down and asked me: "What kind of cake do you want?"

Mom was French and could she ever bake! But she had to ask me because even then I had two favorites. Angel food cake with strawberries and whipped cream was usually my first choice. But yellow cake with dark chocolate frosting was my second choice.

I'm not sure if this birthday cake preference is a genetically programmed thing, but it's almost as if the doctor who delivered me had said to the nurse, "It's a boy! Angel food cake with strawberries! Maybe yellow cake with chocolate frosting. No sprinkles!" The nurse dutifully marked the chart.

So far, I've enjoyed more birthday cakes made especially for me than I care to remember. Fifty-five were angel food cake with strawberries and the rest were yellow cake with chocolate frosting. It would never occur to me to ask for anything else.

My mom baked from scratch, and Dad knew this. She would list angel food cake on the grocery list and dispatch him to the store. She thought he would know that she was expecting him to buy flour, sugar, eggs, and cream of tartar. What she got instead was a box of Betty Crocker Angel Food Cake Mix.

Dad and I were in the living room talking about the Yankees lineup for opening day a couple of weeks away. My hero Mickey Mantle had a lot of trouble with his knees. We were discussing who would play center field if Mickey couldn't start, when a commotion erupted in the kitchen.

"Len, what the hell is this?" Mom yelled as she charged from the kitchen holding the box of cake mix.

"It's fine, dear. It's from Betty Crocker. She's a famous baker. She knows what she's doing," Dad told her. "Look, her photo is on the box."

"You know her?" Mom asked.

"I've seen her around," Dad replied.

Mom stomped back to the kitchen.

I sat nervously on the couch. This was my cake, after all. I was worried.

When he was a kid, my dad saw Lou Gehrig play in

person against the Indians in Cleveland. He knew everything there was to know about every Yankee. So my dad tried to calm me down with tales of sliders, fast balls, and home runs by our beloved Yankees. He talked about Elston Howard, Mickey Mantle, and Roger Maris. By the time we got to Whitey Ford, Tom Tresh, and Bobby Richardson, I had stopped worrying about what was going on in the kitchen.

And then it happened . . .

To this day I remember that shrill scream.

"Oh no! Len, come quick. There's a problem with the cake!"

I was young, I was naive. I didn't know there could be a problem with a cake. What could it be? Could it explode? Could it hurt my mom? I timidly followed Dad. Maybe I could help.

As we approached the oven, we could see that something wasn't right. The cake had risen to fill the whole oven. It was pushing the oven door open. I was afraid that if my dad opened the oven door, my birthday cake would escape.

Dad was calm. He stayed cool. He grabbed the cake box and the phone in one motion. He dialed the phone number on the side of the box as he swung his butt against the oven door to keep it shut.

"Who are you calling?" Mom shouted.

"Betty!" He held his right index finger across his lips, so we would keep quiet.

We could only hear one end of the conversation.

"May I speak to Betty Crocker, please." Betty must have come on the line.

Dad told Betty what was going on in our kitchen.

"Get a pencil and paper," he whispered to me. "I have to write down the instructions."

"Uh-huh, uh-huh. Got it. Got it. Yes, yes, is that it?" he said as he scribbled furiously.

He slammed down the phone and ran to the garage. He returned with his Black and Decker reciprocating saw. He mumbled something about too much yeast as he tentatively opened the oven door.

Out popped the largest angel food cake I had ever seen. It must have been two feet around and six feet long. It was still growing when Dad cut it down to size. I thought to myself: We're going to need more strawberries!

"Why on earth would you buy a Betty Crocker cake mix?" Mom asked incredulously.

"Because Duncan Hines never answers his phone!"

It was the best birthday ever! We had angel food cake 'til Easter.

Two weeks after the great cake event, a huge package arrived. The Betty Crocker Company sent a whole case of angel food cake mix to our house.

There was even a personal note from Betty that read, "Enjoy!"

Lost in Niagara Falls

When you are little, you don't always know many of the street names in your neighborhood. By the time I was ten, I knew I lived on Niagara Avenue in Niagara Falls. I also knew the names Cleveland, South, Weston, and Michigan. I knew 24th Street and Hyde Park Boulevard. That was the extent of my world—six street names—until I won a Lions Club Citizenship Award in fourth grade.

Miss Hazel Smith was a schoolmarm in every sense of the word. She was my fourth-grade teacher. She was tall, had white hair, and wore horn-rimmed glasses. She had a lot of rules in her classroom. One of them was that when you entered her classroom in the morning, you did not go right to your seat. You turned right and entered the cloak room.

I didn't own a cloak. None of my friends did either. None of us even knew what a cloak was. But it didn't matter—you entered the cloak room and hung up your jacket. Even if you didn't have a jacket to hang up, you were not allowed to bypass the cloak room. No one was.

That was the rule.

You entered the classroom and hung a right. Then you walked through this tunnel behind the teacher's desk. It was scary in that room. It was dark, lit only by a single light bulb. The coat hooks on the wall cast scary shadows everywhere.

But the shadows weren't as scary as what awaited us at the other end. As we emerged from the dark, there sat Miss Smith, ready to inspect us.

First we had to place our daily homework on the corner of Miss Smith's desk. If your homework was folded from being in your pocket, you had better flatten it out before you put it on her desk. And if you forgot your homework, you could plan on spending the next hour alone in the cloak room.

After you laid your homework down, you held out both hands in front of her. She checked your fingernails for dirt, and then checked your palms. If you passed this inspection, you got to take your seat.

I always did my homework. Fear is a great motivator, and I wanted to impress my teacher. That year Miss Smith helped me find a skill I didn't know I had. As it turns out, I was the fastest "word looker-upper" in the fourth grade. If you've never played The Dictionary Game, it works like this. The teacher gives every student a dictionary. Then she announces a word and you have to find it in the big book. When you find it, you raise your hand. She calls on you and you announce the page number and read the definition aloud. You get a point for each one you get right. I earned 6,734 points in fourth grade. In fact, my name is still on a plaque on the second floor of Hyde Park Elementary School.

Now it's not that I didn't have really strong competition. Marvin was clearly smarter than me. He always scored 99s on the Iowa Test of Basic Skills, and I only scored 98s. But my fingers worked faster than Marvin's most of the time. I wasn't sure where Iowa was and I never wanted to go there. I was pretty sure that all they did in Iowa was make tests to torment little kids.

Getting back to the game, Marvin wasn't my real competition. Evelyn was. She sat in the third seat from the front in the middle row and was the prettiest girl in the class. She was also the smartest. I had a major league crush on Evelyn, and once I even considered talking to her out loud. I was pretty sure we would get married someday if I could impress her with my dictionary lookup skills.

As many times as I won the contest, though, Evelyn never seemed impressed. In retrospect, maybe I shouldn't have raised my hand so fast and so often. Maybe it wasn't such a good strategy to always look up a word faster than the girl I wanted to marry.

By the end of fourth grade, my fear of Miss Smith had all but disappeared. I caught her smiling at me when I answered her questions. Sometimes she even let me take my seat without inspection. In May, she sent a letter to my parents that confirmed that I had won her over. I had won a "Lions Club Citizenship Award."

Kids from all over the city had won this award, and I'm pretty sure most of us didn't really know why. I suspected it was because I could recite the entire Pledge of Allegiance from memory, but also maybe because of my Dictionary Game skills. The award came with a prize. All the winners got to go to the Strand Theater on Old Falls Street to see a special screening of *The Sound of Music*.

My dad drove me from our home on Niagara Avenue to the movie house on Old Falls Street. That was when I found out how many great citizens there were in Niagara Falls. The theater was packed with kids from all over the city.

The house lights dimmed. The theater grew quiet. Officer Szabo appeared from behind the velvet curtain rolling a brand new Schwinn Sting-Ray bicycle onto the stage.

He announced that he was going to raffle off the bike at intermission. "Hold on to your admission ticket," he told us. All the kids started searching their pockets for their ticket stubs.

Then a magician came on stage and did tricks for us. I don't remember all the tricks, but I remember two of them. A bunch of white doves appeared out of nowhere from the magician's hands and started flying through the theater. One of them pooped in Mary Ann's popcorn. All the boys started to laugh, but Mary Ann didn't think it was funny. We felt sorry for her and gave her some Milk Duds.

The scariest trick, though, involved my good friend, Timmy. He got called up to the stage and then he got himself sawed in half. We were all worried about him because we liked Timmy and wanted to play dodgeball with him again. He just kept smiling through the whole operation though, so we guessed it didn't hurt too much. We were pretty relieved when he walked off the stage on his own two legs.

It doesn't get much better than this for a ten-year-old—free popcorn, free movie, and magic tricks. I didn't win the bike. Some girl from 39th Street School won. That was OK with me because the bike was pink and I wouldn't have ridden it anyway, at least not in the daytime.

The girls all seemed to love the movie, but the boys weren't so sure at first. There were nuns in it after all. There was lots of singing and mushy love stuff too. But we got real interested when the army men showed up and the von Trapp family had to escape by walking over mountains to Switzerland.

Afterward, all the kids waited outside on the sidewalk for our rides home. I waited for my dad as the other kids were picked up until I was the only one left. I waited for a really long time, at least five minutes.

The street sign across from the theater said, "Old Falls Street." I knew I lived in Niagara Falls, and I knew I lived on Niagara Avenue, so I figured I was pretty close to home. It was a sunny day, so I decided to walk home. I remember thinking that if the von Trapp kids could walk all the way from Austria to Switzerland across the Alps I could climb every mountain from the theater to my house.

Getting lost when you are a kid can be scary. But there are different levels of lost.

When your mom takes you to Kmart to get new sneakers and tells you to "stay close," it is not a good idea to wander off to the toy department. I can tell you that from experience. It's not a good idea even if they do have the new 1/32 Eldon Power Pack Slot Car Racetrack with Two Cars Included.

It's especially not a good idea because you could hear an embarrassing announcement over the store's public address system: "Robert Simpson, please come to the service desk. Your mother is waiting for you!"

First, I was lost and had no idea where the service desk was. Second, I was pretty sure that I didn't want my mom to ever find me again, at least not soon.

On the other hand, I was getting hungry. I headed to what I thought was the front of the store where I hoped to find the service desk, but I ended up surrounded by rows and rows of women's underwear.

Then a sales lady asked me a mortifying question: "Can I help you?"

It is not easy for a kid to think of a good answer to this question.

"No thanks, just browsing," I managed to stammer.

When I finally reached the service desk, I learned an important lesson. Moms don't really get mad at their kids when they get lost. They just want to hug you when they find you. This gives you confidence for when you get lost later in life.

As I walked away from the Strand Theater that summer afternoon, I was sure I would be home in an hour. At some point I took a left and ended up on Niagara Street and this buoyed my spirits. I thought I lived on Niagara Avenue, but maybe it was Niagara Street, right? I figured I was close to home.

But the more I walked, the more confused I got. When I got to Portage Road, I wished I had my dictionary—I didn't know what a portage was. All of a sudden, I wasn't on Niagara Street anymore either. I admit I got really scared after I passed Osborne Court and came to Fort Avenue. I didn't know Niagara Falls had a fort, and I wondered if the soldiers were friendly. I hoped they weren't from the army in the movie.

It's an awful feeling when you are a kid lost in a big city. It's not that I didn't pass people on the street that I could ask, but my parents and teachers always told me not to talk to strangers. I would have asked a policeman if I saw one, but I didn't see one. When I passed a stranger,

I just tried to look confident like I knew where I was and where I was going.

Eventually I crossed Ferry and Walnut and Pine, and then I figured out that cross streets had numbers. By seven p.m. I was at Woodlawn and 24th Street. 24th Street was one of the six streets in my vocabulary. I didn't know if I was headed in the right direction, but it was going to get dark, so I just kept walking down 24th.

I got excited when I got to Michigan and 24th, and I started to run. When I got to Weston and 24th and saw

Mark Aiduk's house, I knew where I was!

As I turned the corner at Niagara Avenue and 24th Street, I saw my dad, and he saw me. He was standing at the curb by a police car, showing a policeman my fourth-grade class picture. When the policeman saw me, he handed the picture back to my dad, got in the squad car, and drove away.

I was tired from running and relieved when my dad saw me. My dog Heidi saw me too, and jumped from the front porch and ran to greet me. I fell to my knees in our front yard and let her lick my face. I would tell her all about my adventure later that night.

Dad came over to us and asked, "How did you enjoy the movie?"

"It was swell."

"And how did you enjoy the walk home?" he asked.

"It was kind of a long walk."

My dad never said a word about my poor judgment over dinner—he didn't need to. Years later, I found out that he had arrived at the theater about five minutes after I started my walk. He had stopped on his way to the theater to change a flat tire.

Today I use a GPS to find my way to the grocery store. My wife understands and just smiles.

Spelling Baseball

In Hyde Park elementary school, we had a combined class of fifth and sixth graders taught by the legendary Mrs. Dickerson. The fifth graders were smart, but the sixth graders were smarter. Mrs. D was the kind of teacher who could make you feel invincible.

When I struggled with the Pythagorean theorem, Mrs. D explained it again and again until I mastered it. She convinced me that I would need Pythagoras in my daily life, and she was right. I love triangles. Every time I see one, I calculate the length of its hypotenuse.

Mrs. D seemed omniscient to me. I love the way that word sounds. "Omniscient." It really rolls off the tongue. It's one of many great words I learned from Mrs. D.

Mrs. D seemed to know everything. In the morning, she taught us world history and English grammar. After lunch, it was social studies, science, and math. She even knew about sports and asked us how the Yankees were doing.

There was nothing she didn't know. I was pretty sure

that she sat by a fire at night reading the entire Encyclopedia Britannica. She loved to share her knowledge with us kids. Other than my parents, she was the smartest person I ever knew 'til then, with one possible exception. There was this one special sixth grader—his name was Ralph Paonessa.

Ralph was the kind of kid who just seemed to know everything. He was reciting Maxwell's equations in nursery school. By the time he was in kindergarten, he had mastered Newtonian physics. By the time we became classmates, he was explaining quantum mechanics to the rest of us. I first learned about the Heisenberg uncertainty principle from Ralph in the Hyde Park School cafeteria.

Ralph was always nice about it too. He didn't flaunt his special gifts. We had sort of a big brother—little brother thing going on. He would teach me calculus in the morning and I would teach him how not to get smacked in the butt playing dodgeball in the afternoon.

Ralph's real specialty, though, was spelling baseball, one of the greatest elementary school games ever invented. We usually played it in teams—the girls against the boys.

"Who wants to play spelling baseball?" Mrs. D. would ask.

Every boy's hand would shoot up at once.

"Not again!" the girls would sigh in chorus.

It wasn't that the girls didn't like baseball. And it wasn't that they weren't good spellers. It was because they never won. They couldn't win—because we had Ralph. Sure, they had Peggy and Paula and Evelyn, all good spellers. But Ralph was the Babe Ruth of spelling baseball.

Once the announcement was made, we sprang into action. We pushed our desks and chairs to the sides of the room to make space for the diamond. The boys ran and placed chairs at first base, second base, third base, and home plate. The girls rolled Mrs. D's high-backed chair from behind her desk to the pitcher's mound in the middle. That's where she would pitch the spelling words to her students.

I was the manager of the boys' team, responsible for arranging our lineup. It was an easy job. Ralph was my cleanup hitter. He batted, I mean "spelled," fourth.

Mrs. D had four envelopes. They were labeled singles, doubles, triples, and home runs. Singles were easy—even fourth graders would know some of those. Doubles were harder. We sometimes missed those. You needed to be a solid speller to hit a triple. Many of us struck out trying to hit for extra bases. And home runs? Forget about it! Even high school students couldn't spell those.

Most of our games were blowouts. I felt bad for the girls that we didn't have a five-inning, ten-run rule. But at least they always got to go first. Mrs. D taught us that this was good manners. But one day, one unforgettable day, the girls almost got us.

Mrs. D. tossed them some softballs. "Faucet." "Receive." "Caterpillar." They loaded the bases. Then Peggy hit a home run with "onomatopoeia."

I'm like, "What kind of potato?"

Peggy nailed it. She even used it in a sentence—show-off! This went on all afternoon. By the bottom of the ninth, we were down by seven runs.

Our lead-off speller was Marty. He got to first base with "helicopter." Up next, Marvin advanced the runner with "susceptible." Big Ken was next. Ken was recovering from a broken leg, and I was worried about him.

"Etiquette," Mrs. D. said.

Ken squirmed in his seat, bit his lower lip, and cleared his throat.

"E," he started. "T." "I." "Q." Then he paused at the "q." He knew there would be a "u" after the "q," and he said it. Then he stopped and frowned. He looked at the ceiling, deep in thought, searching for a letter. We waited. He looked down at the floor. Come on, Ken. You can do it.

"E" he said, then finished up quickly. "T." "T." "E."

"Correct," Mrs. D. said.

Ken hobbled down to first base.

Our next two spellers failed miserably. Alan made the first out with "spaghetti." It wasn't his fault; he wasn't Italian. Alfred left out the first "e" in "noticeable." We had two outs.

Up came Ralph. Bases loaded, two outs, bottom of

the ninth, and up comes Ralph. We were down seven runs and Ralph did something unprecedented in the annals of Hyde Park Elementary spelling baseball.

"Mrs. D," he said, "I'll go for a double grand slam!"

Our jaws dropped. No one had ever done that before. Mrs. D. kept the double grand slam words in a special red envelope in her top desk drawer.

As our teacher walked to her desk to retrieve the envelope, I pleaded with our clean-up speller. "Don't risk it Ralph! Even college students don't know how to spell those double grand slam words!"

Under the Official Spelling Baseball Rules, if a student correctly spelled a grand slam word, his team would score four runs. But a double grand slam word was in an entirely different class. These words were taken from the final round of the Scripps National Spelling Bee. These words were impossible to spell. If Ralph got it right, we would score eight runs and win the game, but if he missed it, we would go home losers. Game over!

Ralph winked as he awaited the pitch. There was no changing his mind. He pointed to the imaginary bleachers beyond the chalkboard. He was the Babe after all.

Mrs. D. reached into her special red envelope. We waited. Time stopped. Mrs. D. pulled the word from the envelope. She slowly shook her head as she looked at the word. We waited. Finally, she delivered the pitch:

"Pyopneumoperitoneum."

Are you kidding me?

Ralph closed his eyes. We all held our breath. He looked straight at Peggy as he pronounced it perfectly and used it in a sentence: "Pyopneumoperitoneum. An abnormal presence of gas or pus in the peritoneal cavity."

"Is that cavity in a tooth?" one fifth grader asked.

Ralph sounded like a medical doctor as he explained it to us. I personally decided right then and there that Ralph could remove my appendix if I ever got appendicitis.

And then Ralph spelled it.

He methodically spelled it.

He slowly pronounced all nineteen letters, in order, without hesitation: "P-Y-O-P-N-E-U-M-O-P-E-R-I-T-O-N-E-U-M." Wow!

Mrs. D smiled as Ralph walked twice around the bases. Even the girls applauded as we put the chairs away and carried Ralph on our shoulders to the drinking fountain.

We learned a lot that year from Ralph, and even more from Mrs. D.

Holy Thursday and Ringing the Bells

I sometimes joke that I was born on Holy Thursday, but it wore off. When you grow up in a very Catholic family, and your birthday occasionally falls on Easter Sunday, it never really wears off. It's more than just being a "Cradle Catholic." Growing up in a "Very Catholic" family can be confusing for a little kid, challenging for a teenager, and perplexing for an adult.

I learned my evening prayers as soon as I learned to talk. I could recite the Hail Mary before I even knew who the Blessed Virgin was. The prayers were like poetry to me, even though I didn't know what they meant. I enjoyed their rhythm and cadence, and I knew they were special. I also knew, because my parents told me, that I would go to Heaven if I said my prayers regularly.

My mom taught me that I should pray not only for my friends, but even for those who didn't treat me all that well. As I got older, I said way more prayers for the latter than for the former. I didn't know where Heaven was exactly or what it looked like, but I thought it must be an awful lot like Diffine's Ice Cream Shop, except without a cash register.

My dad always said that if we were too sick to go to Mass we didn't have to, but then we would also be too sick for breakfast. Dad fixed scrambled eggs, toast, and bacon every Sunday after Mass.

I wanted to go to Heaven. I really did. So I tried to do everything that Mom and Dad said I should. That wasn't easy, but I tried hard. Sometimes I was even nice to my two older sisters.

Every Sunday morning Mom dressed me in my "Sunday best" before we headed for noon Mass at Sacred Heart Church. I can still remember the blue blazer, white shirt, and clip-on bow tie I wore every Sunday. The shirt pinched my neck.

We always sat in the fourth pew from the front on the left side. Every family always seemed to sit in their particular pews. It was almost like having assigned seats at school except there weren't any name tags. Catholics must be pretty smart, I figured, if they could find their seats anyway.

It was sure hard for a four-year-old to get through noon Mass.

First, it's really hard to stay awake because it's almost naptime.

Second, when it's time to kneel, you can't really see

over the top of the pew in front of you. That's when you start looking around. You would spot other kids in the same predicament. You would make eye contact and communicate with your own special language. We never actually talked out loud, of course. We wanted to go to Heaven. But we could say a lot with just our eyes.

Why is that boy wearing a robe? And why is he ringing those bells? I just couldn't figure out those bells.

If your parents didn't make you kneel with them, they would let you sit behind them in the pew. You then found yourself looking up face-to-face with the strangers kneeling in the pew behind you.

The kneeling dads never paid us any attention, but the moms and grandmas always smiled at us and sometimes pinched our cheeks. Sacred Heart Church had a hundred rows of pews, and on any given Sunday, there were rows and rows of moms entertaining someone else's kids in the pews ahead of them. It was a communal way of keeping kids quiet in church.

The Catholic Mass was unpredictable. You had to pay attention. You never knew when your parents would suddenly sit down. You could get crushed if you weren't careful.

The scariest part was when everyone got up and went to the front of the church. The mass evacuation always happened right after the bells were rung. My mom told me to stay put. "I'll be right back," she'd whisper, and sometimes she'd leave me with a Tootsie Roll to keep me quiet until she got back.

Speaking of pews, I never really understood that word. They looked like benches to me. Mom used the same word to describe the smell a skunk made in our neighborhood. This Catholic stuff was going to take a lot of figuring out.

My favorite part of the pews were the kneelers. Each one folded up against the pew in front of it. It was so cool. By the time I was seven, I was just tall enough to stretch my legs down and lift the kneeler with my toes. My friends could do this too. But God help you if you lost your grip. Even a small thump could echo like a booming crash, and everyone would stare right at you. It may have been God's house, but He never seemed to help a kid out of a mess like that.

But there was something even worse than the sound of a crashing kneeler. Each pew had a row of spring-loaded hat clip buttons for the men to use. Each one looked just like a doorbell but was impossible to press. So we kids would yank the lever on the button with all our might and then let it rip. Boing. Bo-ing. Bo-iing! Sometimes there would be a chorus of boings followed by a chorus of shushes from the moms.

When we were in second grade, a bus showed up in front of our school every Tuesday at two o'clock. It took all of us Catholic kids to Sacred Heart School for religious education. I loved the bus rides, and not just because we got out of school early. We got to play on the bus all the way to Sacred Heart.

I felt lucky being Catholic. I liked religious education. We had a blue and white covered Baltimore Catechism. I had never been to Baltimore and didn't know what a catechism was either, but I liked the way the word rolled off my tongue.

I tried to memorize every page of my catechism. This was required by the nuns. Nuns didn't wear white robes; they wore black ones. I knew from Roy Rogers that this wasn't good.

Mom explained that they were habits, not robes. That worried me, because Mom had also told me that biting my nails was a bad habit. So what bad habits did the nuns have?

I did like the nuns' names though. Nuns always had two or three pretty names. Sister Mary Kathleen was one of my favorites. Others had names like Mary Margaret, Mary Agnes, and Mary Josephine. There were so many Marys I don't know how they could tell who was who.

We spent the whole school year preparing for our First Confession and First Communion. It was a big deal for us kids, so big that it came with a load of anxiety. We knew it was very, very, very important. We sure didn't want to mess it up.

There were First Communion photos in most

Catholic homes. The boys wore a suit and bow tie. Girls wore white dresses and veils. My friends and I openly wondered if we were maybe getting married to the girls in our class. I was okay with it because I had hopes of ending up with my next-door neighbor Susan anyway. She and I had decided when we were four that we were going to get married. Susan's grandma made homemade ravioli and I really liked ravioli.

Religious education was where I learned that being a good student could backfire. One Tuesday afternoon—and I remember this distinctly—Sister Mary Margaret made a big point of explaining this big new concept.

"God knows all, sees all, hears all!" Her voice deepened and she pointed up, toward Heaven, as she proclaimed this truth. After Sister's proclamation, I went straight to the Baltimore Catechism for verification.

There it was, in print, on page 14, exactly as Sister had said. God really does know, hear, and see everything.

This amazed my friends and me. We had all seen Superman on TV, and we knew he was pretty smart. Superman could hear Lois Lane crying from a mile away. Who had better hearing, God or Superman? We would debate that for years to come.

So imagine my confusion the very next week when Sister Mary Margaret started teaching about the ritual and process of our First Confession.

There was a dark little room at the side of the church called a confessional. We were not to enter if the light was on, because that meant that someone else was in there confessing. And we were not to time how long any of our friends were in that closet either, because some kids take longer than others to remember how many times they pulled their sister's hair.

When it's our turn the action begins. The little panel slides open to display a screen, not like a TV screen, more like a fancy mosquito screen. The dim silhouette of a priest loomed behind the screen.

"Bless me Father, for I have sinned . . ." we'd recite as we wracked our brains, desperately trying to remember our sins to confess. How many times had our moms yelled at us in the past seven years? What had they yelled about? We had to correlate our misdeeds to the list of possible sins the nuns had taught. We had to decide between cardinal and venial sins. That was difficult because, up until then, we had thought a cardinal was a bird.

My brother and I had a good way of keeping our sins straight. I knew I had sinned big-time whenever my mom raised her voice and called me "Robert Paul."

Ditto for my brother when she yelled, "Michael John."

You never want to hear your mom call you by both your first and second names, even if it is later helpful in the confessional.

We faced an obvious question about this scary confession thing. It wasn't the dark confessional, or even the shadowy priest. (I was taking my Cub Scout flashlight just in case). The question was an existential one.

I was a second-grade class leader and I had an obligation to my classmates. As a leader, I was the one to ask the big question. I raised my hand.

"Yes, Robert?"

"Sister Mary Margaret," I asked, "If God knows all, sees all, and hears all, doesn't he already know that I pulled my sister's hair three times in the past two weeks, and that I'm very sorry about it, and that I promised my mom I wouldn't do it again?"

Before she could answer, I hit her with a follow-up.

"Why do I have to tell all my sins to Father Ellis? Wouldn't it be more efficient if I just told God directly what I did and how sorry I was? He can hear me, right?"

I could tell from her deep scowl that I had

struck a nerve. Had I missed something in the Catechism?

Sister didn't address this big question in class. "Come with me," she said, and escorted me down the hall to the office. There I had the first of many personal meetings with Father Ellis. Father Ellis explained things in such a great way that I could later educate my friends on finer theological points.

On the morning of my big First Communion day I had my picture taken with Susan. We really looked like man and wife, even though we were eight years old and kind of short. Just to be safe, as we walked down the aisle at the Mass together, side by side, I whispered to her to remember to say "Amen" and not "I do."

Not long after First Communion, my friend Mark said I should think about becoming an altar boy with him. I had already bonded with Father Ellis during our theology discussions, and it sounded important. It seemed like an honor, in fact, so I said I would.

We practiced for weeks. There was a lot to learn. It's one thing to sit out in the congregation and mess up by sitting when you should be kneeling, or standing when everyone else is sitting. When you were up front everyone followed your lead.

There is a cadence to the Catholic Mass. The timing and order get confusing, and so you must practice and learn. You can't count on the priest to help you out all the time. He has lots of other important things to do, although he will tell you to be seated for the homily.

We did a lot of practicing with Father Ellis and we had it all down. But, somehow, there was a scheduling snafu, and Mark's and my first Mass together as altar boys got scheduled with Father Glynn.

Father Glynn was a monsignor. Mark and I didn't know what that meant but we thought he was a General in the Catholic army. And Father Glynn could say the Lord's Prayer faster than anyone I ever heard. It was a beautiful thing to watch and listen to, but I would still be on "forgiving our trespassers" while he was on the "power and glory."

I worried about trespassing, and never cut across my neighbor's front lawn again after learning that prayer.

Father Glynn couldn't sing the Lord's Prayer very well, but he could say it in either Latin or English. Of course you've never really heard it the way it was intended until you've heard my wife's cousin, Greg Campagna, from Detroit sing it at a wedding. He sang it at mine!

I had trouble keeping up with Father Glynn in our inaugural Mass. As you face the altar from the pews, the priest is behind the altar. During the most sacred part of the Mass, there is an altar boy kneeling on the left and another on the right. Mark and I had different duties. Mark had the water and wine, and I had the bells. At long last, I had the bells!

I loved the bells! I wasn't allowed to play an instrument in school on account of a music teacher who told me that music wasn't one of my God-given gifts. Ringing the bells in church was as close as I would ever get to music. And the bells were beautiful both in appearance and sound.

There were three sets of gold bells suspended radially outward from a common handle. They weren't big and they weren't loud. You really had to shake vigorously to get the right sound, which was a beautiful jingle. We were bringing attention to the consecration of the bread and wine. Timing was critical. You knew when to ring them both from what the priest was saying and by what he was doing.

And then it happened...

I lost track of Father Glynn's words. I was so in the moment that I lost track of what he was saying. I remember him holding the Host over his head. I remember Mark mouthing something from across the altar. Finally, after a really long time, like maybe five seconds,

Father Glynn leaned over to me and whispered loudly and emphatically, "Ring the bells!"

Well, I let loose with a doozie! When Mass had ended, I was pretty sure I would be fired. I would never wear my surplice again. But Father Glynn just took me aside. He told me that I had done a good job.

"Will you know when you should ring the bells next time?" he asked.

I nodded. "Yes. I'll know next time."

"Good," he said with a benign smile.

Mark and I served many Masses together after that. We got to be good friends with all the priests. As we got older, we decided to retire from our altar boy positions and give our younger friends a chance.

I was eventually invited to be a lector, probably because of my sanctuary bell ringing experience. In my senior year of high school, I had the high honor of doing the readings at Midnight Mass at Sacred Heart Church. At the time, I was one of the youngest lectors ever to do that. The fact that Father Glynn had asked me made it extra meaningful to me.

As I finished my readings and the Mass progressed, I glanced over to the young altar boy on the far side of the altar, next to the bells. I said a little private prayer for him. He nailed it - right on cue. The glorious sounds of those bells filled the church. I smiled. It was beautiful. God bless.

The Big Pool

The school bell rang at 3 p.m. on June 21, and the students of Hyde Park Elementary were out for the summer. Next year we sixth graders would head to Gaskill Junior High, but, for now, our thoughts turned to baseball, lemonade, and swimming. By the next summer, we would forget the lemonade and turn our thoughts to girls, baseball, and swimming pools.

And we weren't thinking about the dinky above-ground wading pools in some of our yards, or even the giant pool with a deck that covered Charlie Cantara's whole backyard. We were focused on the Big Pool.

I'm not sure why we called it the Big Pool. I never saw a sign that named it that. Maybe it's because, when you are small, everything looks big. But this swimming pool certainly was big. It was the size of a football field. It was just down the street from the elementary school and halfway to the junior high.

It was a rite of passage in Niagara Falls to be able to walk with your friends to the pool, and a real accomplishment to be able to swim without your older brother or sister coming along as a chaperone.

My mom let me go alone to the pool after I earned my Red Button at school. A Red Button proved that I could hold my breath underwater, and that I could float on my back for 60 seconds. I never told my parents that other kids earned a Green Button, which meant that they could actually swim! My Red Button was good enough to convince Mom to let me go unaccompanied to the Big Pool. I never saw the need to tell her about Green Buttons. And I never, ever, told her there were diving boards.

The Summer of '68 was a scorcher. Kids from the North End headed to the pool to escape the heat, and kids from the South End did the same. We didn't really know each other that summer, although we would get to know each other in Junior High in the fall.

It seemed like every kid in the city was at the Big Pool that summer. You needed five cents to get in. My parents gave me the amazing sum of thirty-five cents a week so I could go to the pool every day. I thought then it was because they loved me—when I became a parent later in life, I appreciated there may have been other reasons too.

Every day that summer, Mark, Steve, Jim, and I would play baseball in the mornings to work up a sweat. After the game, we packed our gloves, swim trunks, and our nickel and headed for the Big Pool. By the time we got to the admission gate, we'd be sweltering and ready for a dip in the cool water.

Our anticipation was tempered with anxiety, though, and not just the kind you get knowing that the deep end was nine feet deep. You see, when you passed through the gate, you were met by a big sign overhead: "Swimmers Must Shower Before Entering Pool!"

The boys went to the left, and the girls to the right. In the locker room, we stowed our valuables, like our baseball gloves. We wore the locker keys around our wrists with an elastic band. It wasn't the showers that made us anxious—it was what lay ahead.

We slowly and reluctantly left the showers and safety of the locker room to face the dreaded foot bath. The boys and girls assembled in a single line. The cool water glistened just ahead. We could see it. We could smell it. We could almost taste it. We just wanted to run and jump in.

But the path to the water took us through a small, dank room with a chlorine-smelling foot bath in the center. The bath was five feet long, five feet wide and five inches deep. No one, and I mean no one, was allowed to enter the Big Pool without first entering the foot bath. Another big sign told you so. Occasionally, someone would try to sneak past the bath. But I never knew anyone who succeeded. The culprit was always apprehended by a lifeguard and the penalty was stiff. If you got caught, you had to go home and come back another day.

The foot bath wasn't the worst of it, though. The tallest, scariest woman I ever saw sat in the corner of that gloomy room. She had muscles like a wrestler and wore a permanent scowl. We called her Mrs. Meany, but not to her face.

Mrs. Meany loomed over a stool with a huge magnifying glass and spotlight clamped above it.

One by one we entered the foot bath, but only when Mrs. Meany said, "Next!"

As we exited the bath, we dutifully placed one foot under her light for inspection. Mrs. Meany would squint

at our toes. After a long, long look she would look up. "Other foot," she would rasp. Mrs. Meany examined our toes under her magnifying glass and big light. We had no idea what she was looking for. I hoped it was just dirt and nothing alive. The girls had nothing to worry about, but we boys learned to keep our toenails cut that summer.

Our biggest fear was being sent back to the showers. That was so embarrassing. It only happened to me once, and that was enough. I remember slinking back to the showers past a line of 50 of my pool mates. They respectfully avoided eye contact, just bowing their heads. I could just imagine what each one of them was thinking. There, but for the grace of God and Ivory Soap, go I.

I wasn't the only one sent back to the showers. It happened to my friend Mark too. "There was enough bleach in that five by five bath to kill all the germs in the city for a year," Mark said that day. "It was tough being sent back to the showers thinking that my feet weren't clean enough to go into a million-gallon pool doused with chlorine. Oh, the stigma of it all! Everyone in the Falls knew my feet were not clean enough for the Big Pool."

One of our worse fears that summer was that our names and faces would appear in the Niagara Falls Gazette over the caption, "Kids With Dirty Feet Sent Home From Big Pool!"

The second we passed Mrs. Meany's inspection, we'd run and jump into the water, usually to the blast of a lifeguard's whistle. "Walk, don't run," was the lifeguard's mantra.

It was a great mystery as to why all the girls gathered on the east side of the pool and all the boys gathered on the west side. Only the bravest of the boys ventured to the middle to meet the girls.

I'm not sure what the girls talked about on their side, and it's a violation of the boys' code of honor to disclose what we talked about, but I do remember us wondering why girls wore two-piece bathing suits and we wore one-piece suits.

"Girls have bigger muscles than we do, and they don't want to make us feel bad by showing them off," Mark once explained. That worked for me.

None of us understood our need to show off for the girls, but we all felt it. We had three ways to show off. The first was to swim the whole width of the pool—underwater. The second was to swim the whole length underwater. This was much harder to do because the pool was packed. You had to swim around a sea of legs, and occasionally one of those legs would kick you. As we swam, we imagined every girl in the sixth grade was watching us. It made no difference that we were under-water and no girl could see us.

The underwater swims were a mere prelude to the third show-off challenge—the diving board!

There was a low board and a high board. It was best to start at low altitude. Cannon balls were fun, but to impress the girls you had to do more. A swan dive off the low board was good, but a flip, or a one and a half off the low board was better. That was my specialty.

But the friends I envied were those who could muster

the courage for the high board. My friend Mark was a master. He would climb the hundred steps to the top—ten stories high. He would slowly walk to the end of the board and survey his realm. I'm sure he could see Canada from there. Then he would slowly back up with supreme confidence. A thousand eyes would follow as he took a running five-step start and made a huge jump up and then down onto the tip of the board. He would spring upward and fly like a swan toward the clouds with outstretched arms, then bring his arms into a point above his head as he plunged into the water with barely a splash. The girls always oohed and aahed as Mark flew, or so we imagined.

It was a beautiful thing to watch Mark fly. It was a time of great fun. It was a time of innocence. We nodded to Mrs. Meany as we left the pool for home. She always said goodbye and smiled at us. She really wasn't that mean.

Sting-Ray Bicycles and José Feliciano Burglar Alarms

By the time I was twelve years old, I was the wheelie-popping, sidewalk-stealing, bicycling terror of Niagara Avenue. That year, as March gave way to April, my parents made my dreams come true. They gave me a brand new, purple metallic Sting-Ray Deluxe bicycle for my birthday. It was made by Schwinn and endorsed by Captain Kangaroo. It had specks of diamonds embedded in the purple paint that twinkled in the sunshine like stars in the night sky. It had a padded purple metallic banana seat and high-rise handlebars. It didn't have a bell. Bells were for girls. My bike had a horn to let you know Mr. Trouble was riding down your street. I loved that bike. I slept with it. I washed and waxed it every day. I couldn't wait for summer to arrive.

My bike lacked a sissy bar, so I added one, as tall as a giraffe. The purpose of a sissy bar is to keep your girlfriend from falling off the back of your banana seat while you are riding her around town. I was sure I would need one of those! Somehow, I never really used it, although I once gave a pretty girl named Maureen Mahoney a ride home from Diffine's Ice Cream Shop on the cross-bar. I can tell you there is nothing better as a teenager than having the blonde hair of a pretty girl blowing in your face on a warm summer night as you pedal down Weston Avenue.

Summer arrived and I let loose. I could hold a wheelie on that bike for a whole city block. I would pedal really fast and do tricks to show off for the girls, both real and imaginary, in my neighborhood. I rode back and forth endlessly by the Wades' house on Cleveland Avenue, but the Wade sisters never came out. No matter—if the girls weren't outside to watch, I would parade my tricks for the neighborhood dogs. I could ride with no hands—that was child's play. I could get it going really fast and then stand on the banana seat and fly like Superman, but not in front of my house, because my mom would ground me. I could do a plank with my hands on the lower part of the handlebars and my toes perched atop the sissy bar. I could even sit backwards on the handlebars with my feet on the banana seat, but not through intersections. As nighttime came, and traffic died down, I would open the window in my bedroom a crack, listen to the thunder of Niagara Falls a few miles away, and drift off to dreams of

Olympic gold for me and my purple metallic Sting-Ray.

About a month into summer, I started to keep my purple metallic beauty in our detached garage overnight. I would polish my bike and then lock it up before I went to bed. I would wave to it from my bedroom window before I turned off the light.

Then one day, one horrible day in July, the unimaginable happened. I went to the garage in the morning to ride my bike, and the door was open, and the bike was gone. Someone had broken into our garage in the middle of the night and stolen my most prized possession. I was heartbroken, of course, and not ashamed to say I shed a tear right then and there.

My parents comforted me. They told me they would buy me a new bike when they could afford to. But I knew they really didn't have the money for that. It sure hurt to lose that bike. My sadness turned to anger, and anger turned to a thought: This was a problem to be solved. I was going to get another bicycle someday and I had to make sure that it would never be stolen.

So I went to work. I waited until my parents went to bed and went into the kitchen cupboard looking for seldom-used appliances. I found a Waring blender and took it to my workshop. I removed some switches. I rebuilt the blender. It became a vacuum cleaner which my mom used for many years. I don't think she ever noticed that you couldn't make smoothies with it anymore.

To prevent further thefts, I designed and built my own homemade burglar alarm. The switches were spring-loaded. I connected one to the big overhead door on our garage, and another to the smaller door. Then, I dug a trench through the backyard from the garage to the house and buried the wires. I ran them through a basement window. I fished them up from the basement through the heating ducts into my bedroom command center.

My command center included a sophisticated electrical network that I had installed complete with an amplifier and tape recorder, all wired to the family TV in the living room, and the HiFi record player in the basement. I mounted two very large and very loud stereo speakers on the garage roof and wired them to a 200 watt amplifier. Did I mention the strobe lights?

Go ahead burglar, make my day! Just try and steal another bike from my garage!

I was almost ready. There was just one last detail. What warning should I play through those big speakers? I would make a sound recording that would scare the bejesus out of any thief. I connected a microphone to my tape recorder. I used the deepest and scariest voice I could muster. "This is the police. You are surrounded. Don't even think about stealing Bob Simpson's bicycle. Come out with your hands up!"

I was sure that would do the trick, but I worried.

What if the tape broke? I needed a backup plan. I needed a backup warning. I needed something really scary.

The only two tapes I owned were eight-tracks. One was an album of the Carpenters' greatest hits. I thought Karen Carpenter singing "Close to You" was not very scary. There is nothing really ominous about why birds suddenly appear or why she won't last a day without you.

But what about that other tape, a José Feliciano album? I listened to the whole thing and decided on the scariest track to thwart any would-be burglar. It was "Light my Fire." Fire is scary, right? I configured my system to play that song loudly and repeatedly. The trap was set. I pushed a big green "pulverize" button, recycled from the blender. My alarm was set at precisely 10 p.m. on Friday night. Then I fell asleep.

I had made one little mistake. I had not told my dad about the new and sophisticated alarm system that I had installed. It never occurred to me to tell him because he never parked his car in the garage.

But on this night, of all nights, he happened to have gone to an awards dinner after work. He'd stayed late at the dinner, really late. He pulled in around 1 a.m. and for some reason decided to park in the garage.

And then it happened . . .

At 1 a.m. on a quiet summer evening on Niagara Avenue, all hell broke loose. When my dad opened the overhead garage door, strobe and flood lights started flashing in our backyard and the house. The TV turned on full blast in the living room. The HiFi in the basement started playing a track from the Herb Alpert and the Tijuana Brass album, *Whipped Cream and Other Delights*. An amplifier pumped the horns through the garage-top speakers. My scariest twelve-year-old voice warned my dad that he was surrounded by the police.

Lights went on in our neighbors' houses. Our phone started to ring. I heard police sirens in the distance. From my bedroom window, to my horror, I saw my dad standing in the garage. He didn't look happy.

And then, as my dad would later recount on many occasions, he was serenaded by José Feliciano telling him to "'come on baby light my fire'—for the whole damn neighborhood to hear!"

It is at these precise moments that a twelve-year-old feels a lot like Theodore Cleaver, and contemplates running away from home and never coming back. As I quickly made a peanut butter and jelly sandwich in our kitchen and planned my escape, my dad came in the back door. He just looked at me and smiled. "Go to your bedroom, turn it off, and get that damn burglar alarm out of my garage first thing in the morning."

A few weeks later, my dad bought me a new bike. I loved my dad.

Delivering the News

My parents got married for richer or poorer. They raised four kids, two older girls and two younger boys. I was the older boy. Whether we were rich or poor was a matter of perspective. My sister Gloria and I felt relatively rich because we, as the older of our respective same-sex siblings, had new clothes and new sneakers. Mary and Michael weren't so sure. They got the hand-me-downs. I felt an obligation to not scuff my shoes or wear holes in my sneakers before I outgrew them. I didn't want my kid brother stuck with stuff that would embarrass him in front of his friends.

One day my dad left his paycheck on the kitchen table and I saw it. Two hundred and fifty dollars! A fortune beyond belief! A hamburger only cost fifteen cents at Henry's. (Frankly, I didn't understand why my dad didn't go there every day. I mean, they had chocolate milkshakes made with real ice cream!)

Once I learned that we were rich, I couldn't understand why my weekly allowance didn't reflect our net worth. I was glad to have my weekly fifty cent stipend, but it barely covered my living expenses, which included a weekly bike ride to the aforementioned Henry's for a hamburger. If I added a milkshake and fries to my order, my allowance was gone in a heartbeat. I was only ten, but I was ambitious. I dreamed of cheeseburgers, fries, and a shake at least twice a week.

My neighborhood friends and I often discussed our dire financial situations. We were all in the same boat, and we launched a number of enterprises to try and improve our condition. One time we even formed a corporation.

Grass cutting, leaf raking, and snow shoveling were great money earners, but that income was seasonal. Errant golf ball retrieval services were particularly lucrative. There were a lot of awful golfers at Hyde Park Golf Course. Of course, you had to be able to swim in Gill Creek to be successful. The neighborhood girls had the lemonade market cornered and we guys just couldn't compete.

A paper route was the holy grail of money-making for a kid in Niagara Falls. If you could get a route, you had a steady source of income. Paper routes were coveted, sometimes handed down in families from brother to brother.

I'm old enough to remember that we were called paperboys. But the feminist era was emerging, and it was only a short time before our lemonade-selling sisters were getting paper routes, and we all became "newspaper carriers."

A kid had two choices in Niagara Falls. You could deliver the Courier-Express if you didn't mind getting up at five in the morning, or you could deliver the Niagara Falls Gazette after school.

What a lot of people don't know is that there are laws about newspaper delivery work. For example, Section 3228 of New York's Education Law defines a "newspaper carrier" as "a minor between the ages of eleven and eighteen years of age who engages in the occupation of delivering, or selling and delivering, newspapers..."

I was pretty sure that the fifth-grade girls would be impressed by a kid who had an "occupation." Before I had an occupation, all I had was a Rawlings first baseman's mitt and a pair of roller skates. Oddly, none of the girls in my class ever asked me what I did for a living.

"If you want to be a paperboy, you will have to know the laws," my mom told me. I had to go to the library to look up the law, and it was a good thing I did, because I found out later in life that they don't teach the paperboy law in law school.

For example, who knew that the law said, "No newspaper carrier shall be engaged in delivering, or selling and delivering, newspapers, shopping papers or periodicals before six o'clock in the morning nor after seven o'clock in the evening or thirty minutes prior to sunset, whichever is later, nor during the time the minor is required to attend upon instruction, nor for more than four hours in any one day when school is in session, nor more than five hours in any one day when school is not in session."

Whoa! It took me almost a week to figure out what that meant. Kids who walk slow, skip school, can't tell time, or don't know when the sun sets are all disqualified from delivering the news. It was then that I decided two things—I wanted to be a lawyer, and I wanted to deliver the news.

The scariest part of the law was in bold print:

"Enforcement. The police shall enforce the provisions of this section . . ."

Wow. A kid could get himself arrested by Officer Szabo if he tried to deliver a newspaper to Mrs. O'Grady 31 minutes after sunset on a Tuesday in July. And God help any kid under the age of eleven caught delivering a newspaper to anybody, anywhere, at any time.

We had lively debates in my neighborhood as to which was worse—not delivering a paper to Mrs. O'Grady or getting arrested by Officer Szabo. We all liked Officer Szabo and figured he would only give us a warning, but Jim Miller definitely worried about rotting in the city jail. "I don't think my dad will post bail," he told me.

It was a proud day when I was approved by the newspaper route authorities and received my Newsboy #6745 badge. The law required me to pin it to the strap of my official newspaper pouch. The badge had to be visible at all times, probably so no one would think I was a mailman.

I was twelve when I got my first Courier-Express route. The Sunday Courier was a gargantuan, multi-section behemoth of a paper. I needed help delivering it on Sunday mornings, so I enticed my kid brother into a criminal conspiracy. I put seven-year-old Mike in the back of the big green Courier-Express wagon and pulled him and the Sunday paper down Hyde Park Boulevard.

"Duck, Mike!" I would yell whenever I saw a car with a cherry on top. I couldn't risk poor Mike getting arrested for underage newspaper delivery, and the only thing worse than that was asking my parents to bail him out.

I was sixteen when I finally landed a prized Niagara Falls Gazette route. I would wait in front of the delicatessen at the corner of 18th Street and Niagara Avenue for the Gazette box truck to pull up with my papers. The truck rolled up promptly at 4 p.m. every afternoon. The driver would lean out the open door and yell, "Read all about it!" as he tossed my bundle of 72 papers onto the sidewalk.

I would cut the twine and start folding. The newspaper tripartite folding method has been passed down from paperboy to paperboy for generations. It has its own special rhythm to it: fold-fold-tuck. Repeat. With all due modesty, I was a natural with the tripartite fold. I could fold a single paper into an effective projectile in 3.6 seconds. That's 72 papers in under five minutes.

We carriers dreamt that newspaper folding and throwing would someday be an Olympic event. Forget about skiing and target shooting. A biathlon is nothing compared to hurling a folded paper from your bicycle onto Mr. Pena's porch, over the head of his sleeping cat, and landing it perfectly-centered atop his milk box. His cat never knew the news had just been delivered.

Of course, most of our customers didn't want us to throw their papers onto their porch. In those days of personal customer service, we knew all our customers by name and where they wanted their paper. We tucked most of them behind a storm door. For some, we had to climb a flight of stairs to an upper flat to place the paper on a landing. Some wanted it left in a milk box, except on Tuesdays, when the milkman delivered the milk. I memorized where every one of my 72 customers wanted their papers placed. I had to know—a college scholarship was on the line!

I loved my customers. The Gazette cost $1.85 a week

back then, and 68 out of 72 of my customers gave me a whole two dollars. "Keep the change," they would say.

We carriers lived for those tips. We knew that we had to give excellent service to get them. We had to get the paper to the right spot on time. If we wanted good tips, we had to make friends with all the neighborhood dogs and slosh through puddles on rainy days or along unshoveled sidewalks on snowy days. You had to get the paper into the slot, behind the storm door, or on the porch, every day before dinnertime.

Some of my customers were especially nice. The Porter sisters were widows in their seventies who shared a home. They would watch for me on cold winter days, peeking out from behind the curtain of their front picture window. As soon as they spotted me at the end of their sidewalk, one would head for the kitchen and the other for the door. As I opened the storm door to place their paper behind it, they would open the inside door.

"Here you go, dear," one sister would say, handing me a steaming mug. "Some hot chocolate will warm you up." And that hot chocolate always had nice fat marshmallows floating on top.

"Here's an oatmeal cookie," the other sister would say. "Enjoy."

"Yes, enjoy," the first sister would say. "Just leave your cup on the porch when you're through."

Those ladies warmed my belly and my heart. They

even gave me twenty-five dollars at Christmas!

Mrs. Haseley was even older than the Porter sisters. She lived alone in a green house on Cleveland Avenue near 18th Street. She was my only customer on Cleveland, but I didn't mind walking an extra block for her. She was 86, and that matched the thermostat setting in her house, summer and winter. She had trouble bending over, so I always rang her doorbell and waited for her to open the door so I could hand her the newspaper. She was sweet to me, and a twenty-five cent tipper, as well.

Delivering the news was an educational experience in more ways than one. I delivered the paper announcing that Neil Armstrong, Buzz Aldrin, and Michael Collins had landed on the moon. I also delivered the news that announced the war in Vietnam was over, and the news that President Nixon resigned. I read every paper I delivered every day.

Every year, the Gazette awarded scholarships to a select number of paperboys. It was the Frank Gannett Newspaper-carrier Scholarship. The year I competed it was a $4,000 scholarship, paid out over four years. Grades were important of course, and you had to write an essay. But the deciding factor, we were told, was customer service.

By this time, I had discovered that $250.00 was not a lot of money, and we weren't rich. If I wanted to go to college, I had to earn the money myself or win a scholarship.

To this day, I don't know which three customers the Gazette called. But I am forever grateful to all of my 72 customers on my Niagara Falls Gazette paper route. I loved them all. They taught me about the importance of hard work, customer service, and meeting deadlines.

I still have the letter informing me that I had won the scholarship.

The scholarship changed my life, but so did my customers.

I think about those days now and then, especially when I read the morning paper. I always tip my carrier. Sometimes I even fold my newspaper just for fun and throw it for my dog to fetch.

The Day My Coach Listened To Me

Sometimes, when I am having trouble falling asleep after a stressful day, I close my eyes and let my thoughts drift to a youth football game I played in on Sunday, October 11, 1970. I was fourteen years old and played offensive end for the Niagara Falls Moose Bulls. We were playing the North Tonawanda 49ers at Colonel Payne Field. It was our fifth game of the season and we were undefeated. Everyone expected us to win, but it didn't look promising early on.

We had a star running back on our team, Bruce Brundidge, joined in the backfield by Larry Williams and Jim Kelley. Our offensive line was big and strong, our defense awesome, and our quarterback, Jeff Kumm, was superb. North Tonawanda's strategy from the opening kickoff was to defend the run and ignore the pass. They stacked the line with ten players, leaving only one safety in the secondary. Our powerful offense was stymied at the line of scrimmage. We were outnumbered and had several three-and-out series to begin the game.

This game was played before the days of two-way radio communication between coach and quarterback, and our hand signals weren't all that sophisticated either. We sent our plays into the huddle by courier—our two offensive ends alternated running in the plays. I was one of those ends and Chuck Powell was the other. Coach Bob Garis would tell us the play he wanted our offense to run, and then we would sprint into the huddle and relay the play to our quarterback.

After getting nowhere running the ball during our first three series, I stood on the sideline during second down with Coach Garis. We watched our star running back get stuffed at the line of scrimmage once again. Coach was worried. He shook his head from side to side. No play he called seemed to work.

And then it happened . . .

"Bobby—what play should we run?"

I looked up in disbelief. He had never asked my advice before, but here it was. I didn't hesitate.

"Well, Coach, I could line up opposite their safety, hold for a one-count, Jeff could fake a hand-off off-center to Bruce, and I could fly down the sideline. If Jeff throws the ball as far as he can, I think we can score."

"Run the play," he said.

"What play?" I asked.

"The one you just told me," he replied.

We had fancy, memorized football names for all our plays. Every player in the backfield had a number. The quarterback was "1," fullback was "2," left halfback was "3," and right halfback was "4." The gaps, or holes, between the offensive linemen were all numbered too. We had dives, sweeps, isos, double isos, counters, and options for our running plays. If Jeff called a "33 dive" he would hand the ball off to Larry who would head for the gap between the left guard and left tackle. We had fancy names for the way the lineman would block. We had cross-blocks and traps. For pass plays, we had screens, curls, down-and-outs, slants, crosses, posts, and fly patterns.

But we had no fancy name for my made-up play, and I had no idea how I was going to explain my idea to Jeff. I raced across the field to tell my quarterback to run my play with no name.

"Fake hand-off to Bruce up the middle, everyone stay in and block, Simpson fly pattern down the sideline for a touchdown," I explained.

Jeff looked at me like I was crazy, as did my teammates. "Did you just make that up, or did the coach really say we should run this?" he asked.

He didn't want to get in trouble.

"Coach told us to run it Jeff, honest," I replied.

Jeff announced the play verbatim in the huddle. Before we broke huddle, Jeff paused and asked me a very important question, "Bobby—which sideline are you going to run down—the left or the right?"

"Whichever one their safety isn't covering," I replied, "Throw the ball as far as you can!"

"Only if you will catch it!" he joked.

The whistle blew, the ball was hiked, and the linemen clashed. Jeff faked a hand-off to Bruce. The defense bought it hook, line, and sinker. I held my block for a one-count, then released and headed for the right sideline. I ran as fast as I could. Peeking over my left shoulder I could see North Tonawanda's safety on the far side of the field. He was completely fooled by the fake hand-off and charged the line. He didn't notice me racing down the sideline.

I ran past Coach Garis, and then by our defensive unit standing on the sidelines. I was in full stride as I came upon the cheerleaders. I thought briefly about stopping to talk to the cheerleaders—they were really cute—but thought the better of it. I could feel their excitement and hear their cheers. I could imagine my parents in the stands, watching me run.

Ten yards, twenty yards, thirty yards, and still no football. Had Jeff been sacked? I would soon be out of range, so I slowed down. It wasn't a track meet after all. I was so alone it felt like I was playing center field.

Then I saw it—a perfect spiral coming my way. It took FOREVER to arrive. I saw the entire North

Tonawanda defense out of the corner of my eye. They all turned to watch me. I could practically hear them wondering, "What? A pass?" The ball seemed to spin in slow motion as I watched it approach. Only a few thoughts entered my mind during those agonizing moments. Catch the ball. Keep your eye on the ball. Watch it in. Catch it before you run. Use your hands, not your body. These were things my coaches had drilled into me.

My whole body trembled as I watched that ball fly.

I slowed down just enough to time the catch. There were 4000 eyes on me as I touched the ball, first with my fingers, and then with my hands—it was hard to handle—it was spinning in the air for a whole 40 yards. I bobbled it for a fraction of a second before getting a firm grip. After I caught the ball, I sprinted down the sideline as fast as I could. The crowd was roaring. I thought about my parents as I ran. I thought about Coach Garis and how he trusted me. It was an 80-yard field. The goal line wasn't marked, and I had outrun the referee.

With no referee to signal a touchdown, I just kept running. Just like Forrest Gump, I just kept running—it felt too good to stop. It was a 60-yard touchdown pass, but I ran a few miles. When I got to Tonawanda, I turned around and jogged back to my team.

There was a big celebration as we took the lead 6-0. Players, coaches, and cheerleaders congratulated me. I tried to enjoy the moment, but I looked for Coach Garis. When I approached him, he was smiling ear to ear.

Coach Garis said only three words to me when I found him on the sideline: "You were right!"

"Thanks, Coach."

After that play, North Tonawanda returned to a normal defense, guarding against the pass. This opened up our running game, Bruce scored three touchdowns, and we went on to win the game 62-0, although it seemed a lot closer on the field. I scored another touchdown but somehow I only remember the details of the first.

It took me many years to figure out why I remembered that game, and that play, so vividly, and why its memory always brings me comfort. It took a long time to figure out that it really wasn't the thrill of scoring a touchdown. It was because it was the first time in my young life that an adult, other than a parent, sought my advice then followed it.

Coach Garis charged me with responsibility that day, and trusted me on behalf of the team. It was more than a play, and more than a game. It was a life lesson. By the time I figured it out, Coach Garis had passed away, and I never got the chance to thank him for the way he treated me, and for the lessons he taught me on that beautiful autumn afternoon. But I think he knew. That's why he did what he did. That's why he gave so freely of his time and talent to young people. Even if I had dropped the ball, I'm pretty sure I know how he would have greeted me on the sideline: "You were right!" he would have said.

I learned two important lessons on the field that day. I learned that it's important to ask the advice of a child under your care, and to follow it if you can. And I learned that if a teacher or coach helps you along the way, you should try and remember to say thank you while you still can.

The Music Man at Gaskill Junior High

A long black limo arrived in front of Gaskill Junior High on April 1, 1971. Out popped the two stars for the premiere of *The Music Man*. Carol Scaletta and Mike Badolato walked hand in hand down the red carpet from Hyde Park Boulevard to the front door of the school. In an hour, Carol would play Marian the Librarian to Mike's Professor Harold Hill.

Thirty sixth-graders from the Hyde Park Elementary School Safety Patrol stood arm in arm on both sides of the carpet to hold back the paparazzi and the parents, grandparents, brothers, sisters, and cousins of every junior high cast member.

There was thunderous applause from the crowd as the whole cast arrived and followed the stars into the school. Light bulbs flashed from the cameras of the photographers of the Niagara Falls Gazette and The Dial, Gaskill's student-run newspaper. The stars entered the school and were quickly ushered backstage under guard by the Safety Patrol.

Each sixth-grader on the Safety Patrol had an official silver whistle and a matching shiny badge pinned to a fluorescent yellow strap that draped his torso diagonally from his right shoulder to a clasp on his belt. Each patrolman had a hand paddle that said "STOP" in red letters on one side and "GO" in green letters on the other. No one messed with the Safety Patrol. If they didn't like you, they could send you into traffic.

Opening night was the culmination of three long months of rehearsals for these young thespians. The sign-up sheet for *The Music Man* at Gaskill Junior High had been posted in January. Every ninth-grader got in line, including me. Talent or not, I had to be a part of the drama club.

But show business is ruthless. I remember watching my classmates in the line ahead singing and dancing their hearts out, only to hear the director say, "Thank you—we'll let you know." This was the equivalent of asking your mom or dad for a new bike and having them say, "We'll see." You were never going to get that bike, and these kids were never going to sing or dance in River City.

I felt happy for my friends who got parts in the play. I felt sad for all the kids who were told they wouldn't get a part. I was mostly happy that I was so far back in the audition line that I could chicken out early and still have time to sign up for the chess club, which is exactly how I became president of the Gaskill Junior High Pawn Pushers.

If the director didn't pick you for a part in the play, there was a good chance he would find something else for you to do. There are twenty-one named characters in *The Music Man*, plus a chorus and a few unnamed extras, not to mention the extensive all-boys marching band. (I'm pretty sure there were girls in that band with long hair tucked under their hats). We had 600 students in our school. There were 30 in the play, 40 in the band, and 529 on the stage crew. I didn't even try out for stage crew—they seemed to have enough kids already.

Then, out of the blue, on March 31, 1971, I got what they call in show business a "big break." My agent called and told me the director had a major problem. Rusty, the red-haired, eighth-grade spotlight operator, had come down with the measles and couldn't perform on opening night. He was probably down for the count. I'm not sure how the director heard about my spotlight skills, but I was hired on the spot. Dress rehearsal went off like a charm—I even used different colored filters to set the mood for different scenes.

I didn't know our stars as well as I should have, considering that I would have the job of shining lights on them on stage. But I knew they were talented. I remember that Mike could sing like Sinatra. And he could act. He had real stage presence and all the girls were crazy about him. Carol was phenomenal. She was one of the two famous Scaletta twins. (Cathy was her sister). They were both very smart, very pretty, and very talented. And they both could sing!

The players all knew their lines, and they were ready. Marty Shimmel, as Marcellus Washburn, was cracking everyone up backstage with his usual humor. He was seen combing white shoe polish into Mike Badolato's hair to make him look older. Mike didn't get that shoe polish out of his hair until eleventh grade. Penny Ferro, as Zaneeta Shinn, and her next door neighbor, Lynne Kukulka, as Mrs. Paroo, were giggling and laughing. Luke Nicolette was polishing the anvils he would be selling on the train. Alma and Ethel were rehearsing, singing about picking a little, talking a little, and cheeping a little.

This was a really big deal. The Niagara Falls Gazette ran a front-page headline in a six-point font about the show. If you squinted really hard, you could read that 100 students took part in the performance, but it felt like the whole school was involved.

We even had bumper stickers printed which we sold for $1.00 each to raise money for the drama club. Some of these are now in the Gaskill Junior High School Drama Club Museum, and Joyce Bennett still has one pasted on her car. My dad wouldn't let me put one on his car. He said this was something we should treasure in a scrapbook.

By 7:45 p.m., everyone had taken their seats and the Gaskill band began to softly play the overture. I took my position behind the main spotlight in the first row of the balcony. I had a list of the scenes on my left with a guide for mood lighting, and a walkie-talkie in my lap so I could coordinate with my lighting staff backstage. As the lights dimmed, I turned on the brightest spotlight in the auditorium and focused it on the gold Gaskill Junior High School logo in the top center of the blue curtain, which was still closed.

The pre-puberty voice of an eighth-grade boy boomed through the packed auditorium: "Ladies and gentlemen, the Gaskill Junior High School Drama Club is pleased to present Meredith Willson's *The Music Man!*"

With that, the band struck up. The music was coming from the hallway behind the audience and not from the orchestra pit. Suddenly, the two side doors to the auditorium sprang open and in marched the Gaskill Junior High Marching Band, in all its glory. The audience went wild as they marched down the aisles on the left and right of the auditorium. I lost count, but I think there were 76 trombonists leading the big parade. These teenage musicians wore sparkling new blue and gold uniforms. Moms, dads, and grandparents smiled with pride.

I got carried away with the music myself and started doing figure eights with my spotlight on the front of the curtain. That was an ad lib sort of thing. The music moved me to do it. If I couldn't dance on stage, at least my spotlight would dance! When they got to the front, the musicians marched up the steps to the stage from opposite sides and then marched toward one another. Trombones, trumpets, and tubas blared. I moved my spotlight back and forth as they marched, and the light reflected from their shiny instruments. By the time they met at center stage, turned and faced the audience, the crowd was on its feet, applauding wildly, and the musical hadn't even started yet.

The performers had won the audience over and they knew it. My classmates sang and danced their hearts out that evening. The parents must have been so proud of their young stars.

In between scenes, the curtain would come down and the stage crew would change the scenery as quickly and quietly as possible while the orchestra played incidental theme music. I always took these opportunities to do figure eights on the curtain with my spotlight. I would also scan the audience with my light, looking for celebrities and talent scouts for my friends.

And then it happened . . .

It was Carol's big scene—her solo. This was the only scene in the whole musical where there were no house lights—just my spotlight—shining on our star singing

"Till There Was You." The curtain came up and Carol walked slowly across the stage to a footbridge over an imaginary stream. Her parents and grandparents were on the edges of their seats in anticipation. The orchestra began to play. I was distracted impressing myself drawing figure eights when the music started to play. And then Carol started to sing, in the dark!

I tried to find her, but the spotlight got stuck pointed at the ceiling. There are four verses in this beautiful love song. She sang the first verse beautifully in total darkness, as I struggled to move the spotlight. She was singing about bells on a hill as I struggled with the spotlight.

By the time Carol finished the first verse, I had put the spotlight back on its mount, and started to look for her. I could hear her. We all could. But finding her on stage was another matter. I looked to the left and then to the right, but I couldn't find that damn bridge. Well, we had trouble my friends, right here in the Gaskill auditorium.

To her credit, Carol was unfazed, and continued to sing. I was preoccupied with the spotlight, but I remember her singing about birds in the sky. At this point, I'm thinking, there may be birds in the sky, and Carol never saw them winging, but at the moment, there's a girl on the stage, and no one is ever going to see her singing.

As I continued the search, someone from the audience yelled up to me. "She's a little to the right!" Others turned on flashlights to show me where she was. The stage began to look like an airport runway.

It was just after the second verse that I found Carol. She smiled as my soft spotlight found her. I sensed her parents smiling too. I felt some relief. Carol sang on about roses, fragrant meadows, dew, and dawn.

As the song came to a close, I slowly tightened the spotlight on Carol's beautiful face. The audience quietly savored the final verse as her voice echoed from the stage to the balcony and back again. The orchestra played its final notes as Carol stood beaming on the footbridge. The audience was speechless and quiet—but only for a moment. Then, suddenly, the entire audience rose to its feet and gave Carol a well-deserved standing ovation. The applause was so loud that most people probably didn't hear the commotion in the first row of the balcony. The director came to visit me. Behind him were my understudies, Anita Ventresca and Laura Mendola. I didn't know spotlight operators had understudies.

I was officially fired from the drama club in the middle of Act II, before the final curtain fell. It was the end of my brief theatrical career. I haven't taken part in any theatrical production since that opening night, but every time I turn on a flashlight, I do a figure eight and remember.

Carol didn't need a spotlight. She sang like an angel. If you were lucky enough to be at that premiere, I'll bet you can still hear her singing in your mind's ear.

Dating in the 70s —The Seven-digit Stutter Step

If you were an eligible girl in the 70s, waiting for that boy to call you and ask you to the school dance, and if the call never came, here is the likely reason why. It wasn't you; it was your phone number. In Niagara Falls, in the days of rotary phones, we all had two-letter prefixes before our five-digit phone numbers. These were called exchanges. The two most common exchanges for us were BU and BE. For a teenager like me, contemplating calling a girl and asking her to the dance, these were just abbreviations in my mind for "BUt she will just say no," or "BE courageous, maybe she will say yes." The absolute worst phone number for a kid to call was BU-00000 or BU-99999. Here's why:

In 1972, it took exactly 1.1 seconds for the rotary dial to return to its starting point when the digit "0" was dialed. I know. I timed it a thousand times when I was 16.

That might not seem like a long time, but I assure you it was an eternity if you were a 16-year-old boy using that phone to call a girl to ask her for a date. That is just enough time for terrible thoughts to enter your mind.

It is also enough time for prayer.

"Please let her answer. She knows I like her. She knows the dance is this Friday."

If not her, "Please let her mother answer." She is kind. Mothers understand.

If not her mother, "Please let her sister answer." Sisters stick together, don't they?

"Please don't let her kid brother answer." He will tease her.

"Please don't let her big brother answer." He will beat me up.

"Please, please, please, don't let her father answer."

"Who are you?" he'll ask. "What are your intentions?"

It was even worse if your intended date lived close by. Let's say, for example, that you lived on Niagara Avenue and 24th Street, and the girl you were calling lived on Cleveland Avenue near 22nd Street. By the time the rotary dial rotated back from zero to start, you could imagine your intended date's father or older brother running over to your house to beat you up.

Getting back to the math and mechanics of rotary phones, it took 1.0 seconds to dial a "9," .9 seconds to dial an "8," .8 seconds to dial a "7," and so on. When you dialed a "0," it seemed to take forever for that rotary dial to stop rotating. So, the lower the number for the seventh and final digit of your phone number, the less time for prayer and terrible thoughts, and the more likely the boy wouldn't cave under pressure and slam the receiver back on its cradle.

If you were dialing a "1," you were screwed—no time to think or chicken out. In other words, the lower the last digit of your phone number, the higher the probability that the boy would complete the call.

Back then, it took real courage to make the call. In most homes, the phone was in the kitchen, where anyone could answer it. When the kitchen phone rang, it was

a big event. After all, it could be a call from Publisher's Clearing House.

Some families even had extensions in different rooms. My friends and I could just imagine that one of those phones—we were pretty sure it was black—was sitting on our prospective date's father's desk where he could answer quickly and scare the bejeebers out of us.

If you were courageous enough to let the call connect, the real waiting began. When you held the receiver up against your ear, it was personal. Each ring was loud, ominous, and scary. Each ring seemed to resonate through the earpiece forever (.16 seconds). Then it repeated endlessly until someone answered. You had enough time to envision what was happening on the other end. Some angry dad was telling his kids to answer the damn phone. Maybe they would, but maybe they wouldn't. Maybe Mom would step in and answer. But maybe Dad, already angry, would answer the phone. Oh, the trepidation of it all!

Now you know why he never called. You also know why cell phones were invented—and it wasn't to make it easier to make a call. They were invented by some guy who used to be a boy who had practiced and perfected the seven-digit stutter step. He undoubtedly wanted all teenage boys to be able to call a girl directly and ask her for a date, with no chance of interception by brothers or fathers.

So if your phone number ended in a digit higher than "5," and if a boy called to ask you for a date, and if your father answered, and if you took that call and went on that date, I hope you married him. He was a courageous boy. He deserved a medal. And he really, really liked you.

The Race

When I was a kid, I loved to run. I ran everywhere and all the time. I ran to school and back home again. The street signs in my neighborhood were just a blur to me. Niagara, Cleveland, South, Weston, Michigan, Linwood, and Willow whizzed by me like clouds to a jet pilot.

I ran to Coulson's Pharmacy on Hyde Park Boulevard just to buy a Nielson's chocolate bar for a dime. I ran to my girlfriend's house on Michigan near 18th Street and ran home even faster when her father's car pulled into the driveway at midnight. I ran all around Goat Island, stirring up the sea gulls and racing them to the brink of the Falls.

I wasn't racing anyone when I ran. I just ran for the fun of it. There is just something exhilarating about running on the sidewalks of your hometown on a warm summer night when you are a kid, running like the wind without a care in the world. I ran when I was awake, and I kept running in my dreams.

In little league, the first time I crossed home plate,

I turned left and headed back for first. My coach didn't catch up with me until I had rounded second and was heading for third—again. He chased me all the way to home plate. He told me to never do that again, but I couldn't see the point in having four bases if you couldn't run around all of them whenever you got a chance.

In football practice, I loved to run laps before practice. Jeff Kumm and I led our Moose Bulls all around Hyde Park in those teenage days. Jeff loved to run as much as I did. He was a better distance runner than I was but he held back and we ran together. The coach used to punish his players by making us run laps, but it wasn't punishment for Jeff and me —we would screw up a pass play just so we could go for a run together.

Most of the guys on my high school football team hated to run, especially the linemen. They were big and the ground shook like a buffalo stampede when they did their practice-ending wind sprints. These sprints were a rite of passage for football players. Coach Cal made us do them to make us strong. But most of us only knew that they made us tired.

The linemen ran first. It took a long time for tackles, centers, and guards to cover a hundred yards. We told jokes and smiled at the cheerleaders while they moseyed along. For linemen, it was more a stroll than a sprint. The linebackers, tight ends, and quarterbacks ran next. They were faster so we told shorter jokes. At last came the running backs, defensive backs, and wide receivers. This was my group. Our sprints would determine the "fastest" on the team. It always came down to Joel and me.

I wasn't faster than Joel. He knew it and I knew it, but I never lost a race to him. He never lost to me either. The first time we had a wind sprint show-down, Joel lined up five yards to my left for our 100-yard dash. We exploded in a burst of speed when the coach blew his whistle. We were fully loaded down with shoulder pads, rubber spiked shoes, and helmets. We were warriors racing down the field in full armor. Our teammates cheered while "Chariots of Fire" played in our heads. We were neck and neck at 40 yards. But at 50 yards, Joel bumped into me and we bounced off one another like billiard balls. At 80 yards, we collided again. Our race ended in a dead tie.

In every succeeding race, the coach moved Joel a little further to my left. We still collided somewhere along the field. When he started 20 yards to my left, we finally ran a sprint without colliding. We reached the finish line side by side—again a dead tie.

We shared a not-so-secret secret. You see, Joel had a medical condition that prevented him from running in a straight line. He told me it was strabismus. He sort of meandered from goal line to goal line. For every 100 yards I ran, he ran 110, and always at an angle.

Joel and I formed a great friendship and a boatload of right triangles running those sprints. It didn't bother him at all that we always tied, and we all marveled at how well he handled his medical condition. He just smiled and laughed and told me he'd "get me next time." We all knew my friend Joel was the fastest cat on the team.

All this running finally paid off one chilly June day at LaSalle Senior High School. We were the junior varsity Power Cats track team. We were the protégés of the stars on the varsity. We looked up to the upperclassmen—Lucius, Eldred, Marty, Jeff, Patrick, Jo-Jo, and Clarence ("June Bug").

Oh, how those guys could run! Oh, how we on the junior varsity wanted to be like them. But our dreams of glory would have to wait. Today we ran against our crosstown rivals, the LaSalle Explorers.

We had trained for months for this meet. We Power Cats started in January inside the high school, carrying each other on our backs up four flights of stairs to strengthen our legs. We even did wheelbarrows to the top floor, climbing each step with our hands and arms while our teammate held our ankles. Baseball players in the gym had it easy compared to the runners and jumpers in the hallways.

My event was the quarter-mile—once around the cinder track. We wore red shorts and gray sleeveless shirts with a Power Cat emblem on our chest. We wore very cool track shoes. They were thin and sleek. Truth be told, they looked like ballerina slippers except for the tiny metal spikes on the soles. We oozed speed. Three Explorers and three Power Cats took our places in staggered starting blocks for the junior varsity quarter-mile that day.

"Runners—take your marks!" the starter yelled, and then paused.

"Set!" he commanded, as the tension mounted, and we raised our hips to the set position.

We exploded from the blocks when the starter's gun sounded. Our tiny spikes collided with the cinders under our feet and kicked them up behind us. If you were slow and fell behind, you risked a cinder being kicked into your face. I never looked down, but I imagined my spikes were making sparks with the cinders below.

Just past the first turn, our staggers melted away as we all headed toward the inner lane. It was a rush of adolescent energy. As we hit the backstretch, I was neck and neck with Ricky, LaSalle's fastest junior varsity quarter-miler. Our teammates were behind us. I stayed on his right shoulder, gauging his stamina. I'm not sure what he was thinking about, but I was seeing the street signs in my neighborhood in my mind's eye. I knew I could take him by the time we got to Weston Avenue, but I didn't want him to know, so I just stayed on his shoulder, making him wonder.

At the final turn, I kicked in my after-burners and left Ricky in the dust. I broke the tape in 58.3 seconds, not bad for a ninth-grader. My opponent finished in a respectable 59.6 seconds, way ahead of the rest of our teammates. We shook hands and headed to the infield to drink Gatorade and rest up for the relay.

As the sun started to set, the varsity ran their final event, the mile relay. Our varsity team had already won their meet by a landslide and the relay meant nothing in the score. No one could compete with Jo-Jo. He broke 50 seconds in the quarter-mile as a freshman and was one of the top quarter-milers in the state by the time he was a senior. How someone so short, and so humble, as my friend Jo-Jo could cover so much ground in so little time was a mystery and a marvel. As great an athlete as he was, he was an even better friend. He took the time after his anchor leg to walk over and wish us luck in our junior varsity race.

Everything was riding on our mile relay. We had to win this final race to win the meet. This race was for all the marbles and the bragging rights in the city.

Willie, Tony, Eddie, and I walked to the starting line in our red sweat suits. We sized up our competition. They did the same. The starter explained the rules. "Have a good race," he said.

And then it happened . . .

Eddie was the tallest kid on the whole team. He was only in 10th grade but he was already six feet five inches tall. He wasn't the fastest runner on the junior varsity, but his legs were so long that all he had to do was move them once and he covered ten yards.

At first, we didn't notice when the four of us removed our sweatpants for the relay race that day. But then we started to hear some chuckling from the opposing team, and this built to a rising crescendo of all-out guffaws and "Oh my's" from the spectators. We glanced over and there he was, tall as a giraffe, our friend, Eddie, buck-naked from the waist down, and smiling ear-to-ear, totally oblivious as he stretched his limbs. But for his jersey and shoes, he was in his birthday suit for all the world to see. It was understandable for Eddie that he didn't notice—it was a long way down from his vantage point. But for the rest of us shorter guys—well—we were sort of face-to-face with Eddie's belly button.

The whole team raced to surround him. The sprinters got there first, then the middle-distance guys, milers, and finally the shot putters and discus throwers. We looked like a tepee—with Eddie peering out like a center pole—still smiling and laughing. One of our fastest sprinters ran to the team bus to retrieve Eddie's shorts while the rest of us shielded him from public view. When our sprinter finally returned, our pole vaulter lashed the shorts to the end of his pole and handed them up to Eddie, who quickly put them on as we dispersed. It was the damnedest spectacle you ever saw at a high school track meet.

I walked over to Eddie and asked him if he was OK to run our race. He just laughed and told me he would probably run a little slower with his shorts on, but he would be fine.

Well, with all the excitement, we almost didn't notice what our sneaky opponents were planning. My teammate Willie noticed it first. Ricky—LaSalle's fastest quarter-miler—was holding the baton. This was unheard of! He should be running the anchor leg—not the lead-off. It was a golden rule in track that your fastest guy ran the anchor, and your second fastest ran the lead-off leg. This could have been a devastating strategic move had we not noticed it. Ricky would have taken a staggering and demoralizing early lead and we might never have recovered. We huddled together quickly as the starter called us to our spots.

"Guys," I said, "just keep his lead to ten yards, and we'll be fine."

Well, Willie did his best, but he was no match for Ricky, and when Willie handed off to Tony, we were behind by ten yards as expected. I could see Eddie getting nervous but I reassured him. Tony was running his ass off, and we weren't losing any ground.

"Eddie," I told him, "just run as fast as you can and keep the distance at ten yards. Don't give up any more ground and we'll be fine. Run like you are bare naked!"

He smiled at me as he took the baton from Tony. It

was almost comical as our six foot five inch Eddie chased down the five foot six inch runner from LaSalle on the back stretch. He didn't catch him, and he didn't even gain on him, but he didn't lose ground either. Eddie ran with all his heart. He was completely out of breath as they rounded the last turn and headed for home. I took my position in the outside lane. We were ten yards behind as I started to run and reached back for the baton from Eddie. It was just then that I decided to break the rules.

I broke into an all-out sprint from the start and chased down LaSalle's anchor leg. I pretended I was racing against Joel in a football wind sprint and I caught up with my opponent at the end of the first turn. This was a big "no-no" for a high school quarter-miler. We didn't have the strength or stamina to sprint the whole quarter-mile. I would certainly hit a wall before the finish line. But we had nothing to lose. We were already behind. To my great surprise, I felt no pain on the backstretch as I hugged my opponent's right shoulder. I decided to stay with him for the entire backstretch, just to make him nervous. I thought about my teammates as I ran.

At the final turn, I saw my dad in the stands. He gave me a big thumbs up. Then I saw Coach Cal. He was yelling encouraging words. All the varsity guys were cheering. I kicked into a gear I didn't know I had. I spotted the finish line and the tape in the distance but feared I would hit the wall before I got there. And then, inexplicably, my mind wandered—to street signs—Niagara, Cleveland, South, Weston, Michigan, Linwood. By the time I got to Willow, I had broken the tape. It was a 56.7 second quarter-mile leg.

Eddie picked me up in his arms. We celebrated for a few seconds and then turned and shook hands with our Explorer friends from across town. They had run a great strategic race that day. We all had.

Nobody mentioned Eddie's wardrobe malfunction on the bus ride home.

A few years ago, the surgeon who replaced my right knee gave me a few dos and don'ts. "You should never run again," he told me.

That made me think about Eddie and my teammates and that long-ago race.

I still run the anchor leg—every night—right after I fall asleep.

A Teacher for the Ages and His Factual Sh!ts

> *Listen, my children, and you shall hear*
> *Of the midnight ride of Paul Revere,*
> *On the eighteenth of April, in Seventy-Five:*
> *Hardly a man is now alive*
> *Who remembers that famous day and year.*

There are exactly 972 words in Henry Wadsworth Longfellow's famous poem "Paul Revere's Ride," and, in 1973, I could recite every one of them, in order, from memory. I could do this because my teacher, Dr. Donald Rohrkaste, asked me to. He asked all of his students to do this. And there were consequences if you couldn't.

We all have our favorite teachers. Doc was mine.

Doc had a smile on his face, a twinkle in his eye, and a Doctor of Divinity degree hanging on the wall in his classroom at Niagara Falls High. I really didn't know what it meant, but I assumed it had something to do with religion. I only knew that he was a good man, with a good heart, who cared about his students. I also knew that none of us had ever experienced teaching methods like those of Doc's.

The local newspaper recognized him as an outstanding teacher. He was a fireball of discipline. He was strict in the classroom, in a Bavarian kind of way. He ruled his classroom with a three-foot-long wood pointer. Most of my friends were afraid of him, and I was too, at first.

American Literature was the first course I took from Doc. We studied the great American authors: Twain, Cooper, Longfellow, and their friends.

Doc played with words and with us—often in a mischievous way that kept our attention. For each author we studied, he would pass out a packet which included a few sheets of paper containing facts about the author and his works. The first time he passed out a packet, we thought we were hearing things.

"Here are your factual sheets," he said, but he pronounced it factual "sh!ts." He pronounced "sh!ts" in such a way that it sounded like he was describing dog poop, or like he had just hit his finger with a hammer.

These sh!ts were packed with information that we were expected to memorize. I spent hours being drilled by my mom on the facts in those sh!ts. Sometimes she'd scold me when I told her it was time to study our sh!ts. More often she'd smile. And, once in a while, she'd actually giggle. By the end of the school year, she knew more about American Literature than I did. My mom really knew her sh!t!

You didn't dare go to Doc's class unprepared. You didn't dare go to his class if you didn't know your sh!t.

Why? Because he had the POINTER. It was three feet long and made of hickory. It was tapered to a point and capped with a pink rubber tip. He grasped it like a fencer holds an epée.

Doc started each class with a roster of students in his left hand and that pointer in his right. He would scan the room looking for a victim. We would all look down as if somehow that would shield us from the inquisition. Looking down didn't help. He always locked in on one of us.

"Ms. DiGregorio," he'd say, "on your feet!" Then a pause. Mary Ann would slide out of her chair and stand up to face the inquisition. Then the question. "Your highn-ASS, would you please tell the class who wrote 'The Song of Hiawatha' and 'Evangeline'?"

"Longfellow?"

"Is that a question or an answer, Ms. DiGregorio?"

"It's an answer, Doctor!"

"Correct! You may be seated."

"Mr. Simpson—on your feet!" It was my turn to face the inquisitor. He held the pointer and nothing else as he started the interrogation. He didn't need the sh!ts himself. He knew his sh!t cold.

He would hold that pointer in both hands. He'd start peppering you with questions from about fifteen feet away and close the distance if you missed one. If you answered a question correctly he wouldn't move. But if you missed a question, he would take one step closer to you and his pointer would get that much closer to your belly. He would even start to move closer if you took too much time thinking about your answer.

"Please tell the class who came in with Haley's Comet and went out with Haley's Comet."

I was stunned. I didn't remember reading anything about astronomy in my sh!ts last evening. I struggled to remember as his pointer loomed.

"Haley?"

He took one step in my direction.

"Wrong, your highn-ASS. It was Samuel Clemens. He was born in 1835. He died in 1910. He told the world that he came in with Haley's Comet and expected to go out with it. Study your sh!t!"

"Mr. Simpson," he continued, "surely you know the first name of Mr. Clemens' wife?"

Becky Thatcher quickly came to mind. I went with that.

"Becky!" I said confidently.

Dan Mitulinsky, sitting behind me, gasped.

My teacher took another dreaded step, and that pointer was looking like a poker.

"Wrong, your highn-ASS. Olivia Langdon Clemens was his wife. Becky Thatcher was Tom Sawyer's girlfriend. Don't confuse factual sh!t with fictional sh!t!"

"Mr. Simpson," he asked, "enlighten us as to the pen

name of Samuel Langhorne Clemens."

My teacher had a heart after all.

"Mark Twain," I replied, as Doc smiled, the bell rang, and I was able to escape.

How on earth did a teacher get away with all that swearing? With a twinkle in his eye—that's how. His methods worked. It was actually a lot of fun to study sh!t. Even 45 years later, I remember that Jack London brought local color into his short stories, and O. Henry was known for his surprise endings. I know all about Haley's Comet too!

I survived that first course, and later took courses in Shakespeare from the Doc. I would have taken any course he chose to teach.

To this day, I study my factual sh!t.

To this day, I can recite the last verse of Longfellow's poem from memory:

> *For, borne on the night-wind of the past,*
> *Through all our history, to the last,*
> *In the hour of darkness and peril and need,*
> *The people will waken and listen to hear*
> *The hurrying hoof-beat of that steed,*
> *And the midnight message of Paul Revere.*

To this day, I can remember how Doc introduced us to Shakespeare's first tragedy, Titus Andronicus. He picked up his pointer, walked to the door, looked out into the hall to make sure no school administrator was listening, then closed the door quietly. He looked up, engaged us with a conspiratorial gaze and moved closer to his desk. He raised his pointer toward the ceiling.

"Today," he intoned, "I'm going to tell you about Tight-ASS Andronicus, a great Roman general and Shakespeare's protagonist."

It's Academic

Every day at precisely noon, the school bell rang at Hyde Park Elementary and all the kids bolted out the front doors and headed home for lunch. It was exactly four blocks from my school to my house on Niagara Avenue. I raced down Hyde Park Boulevard, crossing Michigan, Weston, South, and Cleveland Avenues. When I got to the alley between Cleveland and Niagara, I took a left and bolted down the homestretch. I opened the gate next to our garage and ran across the lawn. As I opened the side door and climbed the stairs into the kitchen, my tall, beautiful mom was there waiting for me by the stove, always with a big smile.

I jumped into my seat at the kitchen table, facing the living room. My mom always made my favorite lunch for me—a grilled cheese sandwich with Kraft American cheese—all gooey between the toasted bread. Campbell's tomato soup with oyster crackers sat nearby. Mom sat down next to me. She had wheeled the cart holding our General Electric 19 inch black and white television from the living room into the kitchen. A few minutes before noon, she turned it on so we could watch together.

Don Pardo announced, "This is Jeopardy!" as I raced down the alley. I never heard him. My mom announced the categories for Single Jeopardy as I walked across the kitchen. I always hoped they would ask about Sports, Science, and Potent Potables.

My mom was smart. She knew a lot of the "questions," but I was faster than she was, or at least that's what she led me to believe. They gave away $10-$20-$30-$40-$50 just for knowing stuff in Single Jeopardy, and double that in Double Jeopardy. You could get rich in 30 minutes playing Jeopardy! I dreamed of buying new bikes for every kid in the neighborhood with my winnings.

Whenever a contestant would hit a Daily Double, Don Fleming would ask how much they wanted to wager. Before they could answer, my mom would yell, "$10,000" and then I would yell, "$20,000!" We would always go for broke with our imaginary money.

I always won those Jeopardy games with my mom. I suspect that she would sometimes fail to put her response in the form of a question so I would win. Moms do things like that for their kids.

Mom would put a bowl of homemade chocolate pudding with whipped cream on the table as the final answer was revealed and the Jeopardy thinking song started to play. I wrote down my question and my mom wrote down hers. I stood by the door and waited to see if I got it right. As soon as I knew, I bolted out the door and sprinted back to school. I was always a few minutes late but my teachers didn't seem to mind. I think they knew I was being home-schooled.

Jeopardy with Mom was my key to academic success. Most kids don't know this, but a lot of questions on teachers' tests in school are taken directly from Jeopardy.

By the time I got to high school, all those Jeopardy questions paid off. My social studies teacher, Mr. Marsh, nominated me to try out for the television quiz show *It's Academic* on Channel 4 with Van Miller. About 30 of us went to the studio on Elmwood Avenue for the audition. They gave us each a paddle with a number on it. An announcer stood on a podium and asked us questions. Someone kept track of whose paddle went up first and how many answers you got right. For some reason, I always put my responses in the form of a question, but they didn't hold that against me.

A few days later, I was informed that I was one of six students named to the Niagara Falls High School *It's Academic* team, and I ran all the way home from school to tell my mom. My mom told me how proud she was of me for making the team, and I thanked her for making me all those sandwiches and playing Jeopardy with me.

For the next few months, the six of us—two Michaels, Stephanie, Loralee, Mark, and me—practiced for the show with our advisor, Mr. Brass. We answered test questions twice a week for a couple of hours after school. We even had push buttons and buzzers! My team members were all so smart! I wasn't the only kid who watched Jeopardy with his mom.

Mr. Brass announced the final team in January. He named me the captain! I got to sit in the middle and listen to answers from my teammates on my left and right, and then speak them into the microphone on the show. Michael and Stephanie were a lot smarter than I was, so my job was pretty easy.

We had such a great, balanced team. One of us knew Latin, one knew French, and one of us knew Spanish. One of us was strong in science and math, one was strong in history, and one was strong in English. I was especially strong in Potent Potables. We felt pretty comfortable about our chances.

And then it happened . . .

On January 21, 1974, Mr. Brass handed us each an envelope from the TV station. Inside the envelope were four admission tickets for the taping of the show, and instructions to arrive at the station no later than 10 a.m. on Saturday, February 23, 1974. The tickets weren't for me. They were for our family members so they could watch the show live in the studio.

I showed the tickets to my mom at dinner that evening. I could tell immediately that something was wrong.

She handed me a letter from Rochester Institute of Technology that had arrived that very day.

"Congratulations! You qualify as one of the outstanding new freshmen admitted to RIT for next fall, and thus have earned an invitation to compete in our 1974 RIT – Outstanding Freshman Scholar Award Competition …. The competition will be held here on the RIT campus the last weekend in February – Feb. 22-23."

I almost spit out my chocolate pudding. RIT was my dream school. It was the only college I had applied to. My parents really couldn't afford to send me there. I needed that scholarship. Now I had to decide. Should I represent my school on TV or go to the college and compete for a scholarship?

I didn't even get a chance to ask my mom for advice. She knew what I was thinking. She just smiled. "Follow your heart. Whatever you decide to do will be the right choice."

The next day, I went to Mr. Brass' classroom to ask for advice. He was crestfallen. He called the TV station and asked if they could change the taping date.

"No can do!" was the reply. "Too many logistics issues. He can either come to the taping or you can send an alternate. But tell us soon because we have to make nameplates for your team."

Then Mr. Brass called the college. Same response. There was no way they could fairly let me take the scholarship test another day. I was close to tears.

Mr. Brass assured me that whatever I decided was fine with him.

I left Mr Brass and went straight to my guidance counselor, Mr. Laurrie. If anyone needed guidance, it was me. Mr. Bob Laurrie was my best friend on the faculty and my mentor during high school. He was always looking out for me. He knew how badly I wanted to go to college and he helped me every step along the way. He helped me win scholarships and awards and encouraged me to study hard. I knew I could count on him for sound advice.

After I explained the situation, he looked me square in the eyes. "Bob, I can't make this decision for you. This is one you have to make on your own. Follow your heart!"

What was it with all these adults? I wondered. Every one of them is telling me to follow my heart. I had no idea what that even meant.

So there I was. Do I do what is clearly in my own best interest and take the scholarship test? Or do I go on the TV quiz show I've been preparing for my whole life, and do my best for my team and my school?

I did what I do with every big decision in my life. I took a stroll around Goat Island. If I was going to follow my heart, I had to find it first, and I was pretty sure I would find it on Goat Island. I walked the trail and watched the seagulls take flight. Halfway around I decided what I would do. There would be plenty of tests in my life, but only one chance to go on television with my friends and represent my school.

We arrived at the studio at 10 a.m. We all had the jitters. There were big cameras and bright lights. We had big contestant chairs behind our team podiums with our names on nameplates so our parents could tell who we were. We each had our own microphone. We each had a big red button to push if we knew an answer. There was a live studio audience.

Nichols, Newfane, and Niagara Falls would compete for school pride and bragging rights that day.

I took an immediate liking to the Newfane team, and not just because they were all pretty and smart girls. It was because they were just plain nice, and admitted that they were as scared as we were.

I have nothing against private schools in general, or Nichols in particular. But I took an immediate dislike to the Nichols' team captain that morning. I don't remember his name, but I think it was something like Reginald Humphrey Carston III. He wore a blue suit and a red bowtie.

He was pleasant enough as he greeted me by tapping me on the shoulder and inquiring, "First time on the quiz show, old chap?"

"Uh, yeah, and you?"

"This is my second time around. I answered so many

tough questions last year they brought me back again as team captain."

I was wondering just how many years young Reginald had spent in high school, but, before I could ask him, he comforted me with, "No worries, friend, your nerves will calm down by the second or third commercial break."

We scored a couple hundred points in the first round, and were trailing Nichols but barely ahead of Newfane. We lost ground in the second round and fell way behind both of our rivals. I knew we were in trouble when we inexplicably answered "Martha Washington" to the question, "Who was First Lady when Franklin Roosevelt was President?"

It's funny how quiz shows go. We knew the answer to every question Van Miller asked our opponents, but hardly any that he asked us. By the end of the second round, we knew it was hopeless.

It was then, during the commercial break before the grab-bag round, that the thought came to me. If I was blowing a college scholarship in the Channel 4 studio on Elmwood Avenue that morning, it had to be for a good reason.

I ran my idea by Mike and Stephanie and they climbed on board. We HAD to help Newfane win! In poker they

call it a "tell." On *It's Academic*, it's called a twitchy finger. We had full view of the Nichols' student hands on their buzzers. We could sense when they knew an answer. They were smart and they were fast. In all honesty, they were maybe the best team. It wasn't that we didn't like them, it was just that we all really liked the Newfane girls more.

So, every time we heard a question in the grab bag, we didn't answer if we thought Newfane would, and we quickly buzzed in without a clue if it looked like Nichols did, to give Newfane more time.

For example, if Van asked, "What's the capital of New York?" and it looked like Reginald was going to push his button, we would quickly ring in with, "Albuquerque." I'm not saying this was a fair or nice thing to do, and I have mixed feelings about it even today. Sure, there wasn't anything in the rules about it, and we only probably affected three or four questions, but I'm not entirely proud of my behavior that day.

We finished with 60 points on *It's Academic*, one of the lowest scores ever recorded by a Niagara Falls High School team to that point in time. Nichols finished with 420. The Newfane girls won the game with the last question in the grab bag, with 430 points. I still remember the smiles on their faces as they celebrated their win. They really did earn it. As much as we tried, we really didn't affect the outcome.

I'm not sure where Reginald ended up, but I wish him well. He is most likely a neurosurgeon, and I am hopeful that his memory of that day has faded and, if not, that I never require his services.

About a week after the taping, I received a letter in the mail from RIT. It was a personal letter from the Dean of Engineering. He explained that he understood how difficult it was for me to make the decision to represent my school instead of competing for a scholarship, so they decided to give me a scholarship for my first two years of college anyway.

My classmates at school were very understanding about our defeat. They were raised that way.

As for me, I never regretted following my heart.

What Are Clouds Made Of?

Like all little boys, I often lay in the grass in my backyard on Jerauld Avenue trying to figure out where all the ants were running to. I never figured it out, so I turned my gaze skyward and wondered what clouds were made of. Were they soft like cotton? Could you bounce up and down on them like you could on a mattress? Could you put a scoop of clouds on some pancakes with maple syrup and have them for breakfast?

It's funny how thoughts and questions like these get planted in a kid's brain and then lay dormant for years. You get distracted by baseball games in the sandlot, grilled cheese sandwiches and tomato soup that your mom makes you for lunch, and Mrs. Brown's kindergarten stories just before nap time, but the questions you have as a boy never really leave you.

In the summer of 1976, I thought I had left all those boyhood questions behind me. I had two years of college by then. I knew calculus and differential equations. I had read Twain and Shakespeare. I had held a girl's hand and even kissed her on the lips. I felt pretty confident in what I knew and what I had accomplished. But I didn't know everything. I didn't know what clouds were made of.

It was at a college party that I first met Ann. She was tall and she was pretty, for sure, but that isn't what intrigued me about her. In our very first conversation, she told me. It came out of the blue, literally and figuratively. She knew what clouds were made of. She had touched them.

A memory sprang from my brain and jolted my imagination. I just had to know, and she was the girl to tell me. You see, Ann was a skydiver. She had done it a thousand times. She had jumped from a plane and held hands with her friends as they fell from the sky. She had jumped from 3,000, 5,000, and 10,000 feet. Not only had she seen clouds, she had played in them. They were her friends.

We went on a few dates. We enjoyed pizza and soft drinks and a few beers here on earth. I held her hand as we strolled. I think she wanted me to kiss her. And it's not that the thought didn't enter my mind. It's just that the thought of those clouds kept getting in the way. I just had to hear more.

After about a month, it happened. She asked ME on a date. And it wasn't your typical "movie and a pizza" date. She surprised me and took me to her skydiving club. She told me to bring $65—$15 for the training and $50 for the jump.

We arrived at the club on a Friday morning, which met in a barn in Hamlin, New York. She introduced me to Joe, the jump master. Joe was on crutches that day, which unnerved me a bit. He had a clipboard with a pad on it, and my name was on the pad. Right under the pad was a liability waiver form—in triplicate. I gave Joe my money, identified my next of kin, signed the form, and then headed to the barn for training.

If you have never trained to jump out of an airplane, you are probably smarter than I am, but that's beside the point. Let me tell you—skydiving training is very hard and very intense, and a refrigerator is involved. You get an awful lot of training for $15. There's a written exam, a verbal exam, and a physical exam.

And they did it sort of backwards at this club. They started with the landing. I guess they were optimists. It seemed to me a lot like learning how to play chess by studying the endgame first, but who was I to question them. After all, they had jumped out of airplanes and lived to tell about it.

The first thing they did was strap a parachute on my back, show me where the rip cord was, and tell me not to pull it. I thought it was a very good idea knowing where the rip cord was, but I remember hoping that they would also tell me when I should pull it. Then they walked me over to a step ladder next to a refrigerator. And it wasn't one of those mini-refrigerators that you find in college dorm rooms. This was a full-sized Sears and Roebuck refrigerator with an ice maker. It was white. Somehow it didn't seem out of place in the middle of a field next to a barn.

Once you stepped on the ladder rungs, there was no turning back. There was a line of equally crazy people behind you awaiting their turn—sort of like climbing the ladder to a diving board at a swimming pool. I climbed to the top of the ladder, and Joe instructed me to stand atop the fridge.

He used a bull-horn to shout instructions. "Keep your eyes straight ahead and your legs and feet together. Jump off the fridge! When you hit the ground, roll. DON'T LOOK DOWN!"

I was pretty sure I misheard him, and was totally confused as to how jumping off a refrigerator would be helpful to me after I jumped out of a plane.

So I cupped my ear and said, "Say again!" He looked annoyed and repeated himself.

I saw Ann nod her head in approval and mouth, "Do it!"

He didn't have to ask me again. I jumped from a distance of six feet, didn't look down, and rolled on impact. We did this for an hour. I counted 30 "jump and rolls" from atop the fridge.

I felt really proud of my accomplishments in fridge-jumping. I was pretty sure I could jump off any major kitchen appliance after my training. I thought he should give me a certificate or maybe a badge. But he didn't. Instead, he walked me into the barn and attached my chute harness to some overhead cables. Then, with a winch, he hoisted me 40 feet into the air, and suspended me from the rafters. This time I was wearing a helmet with a two way radio.

Joe shouted emergency commands into the radio: "Mae West." "Streamer." "Turn right." "Turn left." And so on.

You had to know what to do in each case. A Mae West meant your chute opened in a funny way that resembled the shape of a very large brassiere. Some students called this a "figure eight," but if I was going down, I preferred the image of a blonde beauty's brassiere.

A chute in the shape of a Mae West meant you were falling faster than you should be. With a Mae West, someone on the ground would assess your descent rate, calculate the number of likely broken bones upon impact, and then advise you to just keep going or eject the main chute and engage your reserve.

A Streamer was more serious. If you happened to look up before you reached terminal velocity, and noticed your chute spiraling like a half-cooked spaghetti strand in a strong wind, you could listen to instructions if you wanted to, but it was probably a better idea to just eject your main chute and pull the rip cord on the reserve. In either case, I was sure glad they gave me a helmet!

After six hours of jumping off a refrigerator, hanging from the rafters in a barn, and studying the contours of Mae West's brassiere, I was ready. But there were two more instructions.

The first was, after you were out on the wing, DO NOT, under any circumstances, chicken out and try to come back inside the plane. If you do, your chute will certainly open, and then suck you, and everyone else in the plane, out into the atmosphere.

The second was, after you jump off the wing, count one-Mississippi, two-Mississippi, three-Mississippi, and then look up to see if your chute opened. That seemed like a good idea to me. If your chute didn't open, we were to await further instructions from the ground. I hoped they would speak those instructions quickly. With these sobering thoughts in mind, and with my last will and testament signed and notarized, we taxied down the runway.

Did I mention that I had never been in a plane before? That's right, the first time I ever flew in a perfectly good plane, I jumped out. And my wife married me anyway. Of course I didn't tell her this story until after the honeymoon.

Once we reached our jumping altitude of 3,000 feet, the jump master called my name. I presume he called my name first because I scored the highest on fridge-jumping.

"Simpson, out on the wing!" came the command.

We were flying at 85 miles per hour as I carefully placed my feet and hands on the struts. It felt like speeding on the highway in a convertible, except knowing that a state trooper wouldn't pull you over.

Once I was stable, Joe yelled, "Jump!"

Off the wing backwards I sprang—spread eagle, hoping the static line would pull my chute open. I was flying, and it was the thrill of a lifetime. It was so exhilarating that I totally screwed up. I forgot to count! I got so caught up in the moment I forgot to count "one-two-three Mississippi."

What to do? I had to think quickly. I briefly hoped that the counting part was not critical to chute deployment. I quickly alphabetized the states in the United States and considered each one. California was too long. Massachusetts was too hard to spell. Fortunately, I recalled that Idaho had only three syllables. I counted, as fast as I could, "One-Idaho, two-Idaho . . ." but, by the time I got to Boise, the chute opened. Whew!

When my friends ask me what it is like to jump out of an airplane, I tell them this: "Close your eyes and don't say a word. Think of all the things you have done in your life. Think of all the things that have brought you joy and brought you pleasure. Throw in ecstasy if you want to. Now bring whatever the most pleasurable thing you ever did to the top of your list and tip of your tongue, but don't say it. Now move that thought down to number four."

And now I'll tell you what the top three really are, in ascending order. The third best feeling in the world is the thrill of jumping out of an airplane and flying like a bird toward the earth. There is nothing like it. No roller coaster even comes close.

But this feeling, as great as it is, is far surpassed by the second-best feeling, which is the simultaneous jolt and joy you feel when your parachute opens.

And the best feeling in the world? It's not what you might think. It's floating down to earth with a parachute over your head, floating through the clouds and looking out over Lake Ontario if you are lucky like I was. For a special treat, jump with a short stack of pancakes and a bottle of New York maple syrup and bring a spoon. As you pass through the clouds, ladle some of that soft white stuff atop your pancakes, and enjoy the ride.

After my first, and only, jump from an airplane, I went home to Niagara Falls for the weekend.

My mom asked, "How was your weekend, Bob?"

"It was fine, Mom, I jumped out of an airplane and learned what clouds were made of."

"That's nice," she said as she put some pancakes on the table in front of me. "Please don't ever do that again." I promised her I wouldn't.

I kept my promise. I went out into our backyard, lay

in the grass, and watched the clouds above.

Sadly, after that first jump, Ann and I drifted apart. Well actually, I stayed where I was, but she drifted out over Lake Ontario after a jump from 10,000 feet and was last seen headed toward Algonquin Provincial Park in Northern Ontario. Boy, that girl could fly!

I would tell you more, but I'm following some ants in my backyard right now.

Fast Food Cashiers and Microphones

I left my hometown of Niagara Falls in 1982 for a new job in Northern Kentucky across the Ohio River from Cincinnati. At first, I didn't know where the closest grocery store was, let alone any restaurants. I was hungry. I wanted pizza. I dreamed of my hometown pizzerias like Buzzy's, Sammy's, and Ventry's.

It turns out they don't eat much pizza in Cincinnati. They eat chili, which they serve over spaghetti with cheddar cheese, diced onions, and oyster crackers. It's really very good, but it's not pizza.

So I went for a drive down Old Dixie Highway looking for a place to get a meal. I passed a few unemployed pepperoni salesmen along the way. The first place I saw was Tom's Mexican Taco Joint. That sounded authentic to me so I pulled in.

The place was huge with a lot of tables and chairs. There must have been a festival in town that day, though, because no one was sitting at any of the tables. A colorful—and extensive—menu stretched above the counter. There were three menu items to choose from and an army of Mexican culinary experts in the kitchen ready to serve. All fifteen of them, plus the cashier, were staring at me as I perused the menu. I studied it carefully. It was a tough choice, deciding between a taco, burrito, or empanada.

I approached the cashier, whose name was Anna Pullano Bongiovanni, to place my order. All of her colleagues stood at attention, eyes focused on me, anxiously awaiting my decision.

Now, picture this: Her colleagues in the kitchen were literally six feet behind Anna. She had a microphone at her disposal next to the cash register. It was mounted at the tip of one of those flexible coiled silver metal stands.

Anna could bend that coiled mike stand into any

shape she wanted. She could probably have bent it into that balloon art classic, a dachshund, like an artist at a kid's birthday party.

Mark Twain had a perfect description of a dachshund. He called it a "long, low dog, with very short, strange legs—legs that curved inboard, something like parentheses turned the wrong way."

I might add that this particular dog has a tiny head that barks, and it takes him a very long time to turn a corner.

Anna slowly and deliberately pulled the microphone close to her mouth.

"May I help you?" she boomed, shaking the walls.

I was taken aback by such a large sound from such a petite cashier. I timidly approached her to place my order.

"I'll have a taco please."

The kitchen army must have heard me. They gave me knowing looks and scurried off to do their thing.

But it made no difference to Anna. She slowly brought her lips to within a few millimeters of the windscreen on the microphone. In her best professional wrestling announcer voice, she boomed again: "One soft-shell beef taco!"

I asked her for a side of guacamole just to hear her make another announcement.

"Add guacamole," echoed down the Ohio River valley

all the way to Louisville.

The deafening sound of Anna's description of my taco order filled the restaurant. It reverberated like the song of a yodeler in the Swiss Alps. I thought I felt the vibration of the John A. Roebling Suspension Bridge as it started to sway across the Ohio River. I'm pretty sure they heard my order at the Grand Ole Opry down in Nashville, Tennessee.

Then, still leaning into the microphone while looking me straight in the eye from two feet away, she bellowed again: "Your order number is 67!"

I looked at Anna, then to the left, then to the right, then over my shoulder, as I wondered where the other 66 customers had gone. I wondered if they were locked in the freezer!

Anna and I were so close to one another that she could have whispered my number to me. I would have heard it. I was close enough to read her lips. But I was glad she boomed it. It made me feel important.

I took my receipt and sat myself down in the middle of a bench, ten feet away from the cashier.

Anna and I traded awkward smiles for ten long minutes as my taco was being prepared. No new customers arrived. It was just me, Anna, and the kitchen army. They started to feel like family, sort of.

Eventually my taco was ready. The head cook handed it into the glove-wrapped hands of an assistant. She carefully wrapped it in paper, then passed it on to a young man—a kid, really—who carefully put it into a paper bag. The kid passed the bag to an even younger kid—a boy really—who added a plastic container of guacamole to the bag. The boy gave the bag to an older guy whose shirt pocket was embroidered "Manager." The manager carried the bag across a distance of at least four feet and placed it on the counter in front of Anna.

Anna grabbed the bag, cleared her throat, and pulled the microphone close.

"Number 67, your order is ready!"

She repeated this: "Number 67, your order is ready!"

I again looked to my left and to my right. I didn't want to take someone else's food after all.

I stood up, approached the counter, and handed Anna my receipt.

She took it from my hand, put on a pair of reading glasses, and studied that receipt. Only after careful examination did she hand me my taco.

It was then that I simply couldn't take it anymore. I couldn't resist. I totally lost it. I leaned over the counter. I grabbed her microphone, pulled it close, cleared my throat, and boomed: "THANK YOU!"

They all smiled and nodded.

I went back to Tom's Mexican Taco Joint the following Saturday, and ordered a burrito. My number was 68. I enjoyed my burrito alone in the restaurant.

Two years later, I moved back to Niagara Falls. Shortly after my return, I stopped by Sammy's Pizzeria at Hyde Park Boulevard and Pierce Avenue. I hadn't been there in a couple of years, but I had been a regular customer before I left town. I ordered a cheese and pepperoni pizza for takeout, and took a seat to wait.

Fifteen minutes later, with no microphone, the cashier leaned over and said, "Bob, your pizza is ready."

It's great to be home, I thought, where everybody knows your name.

Is He Rehabilitatable?

It wasn't until I had been married for a while that I learned that mothers and daughters share a secret language. Even then, I didn't learn the depth of that language until I had a daughter of my own. This secret language contains words, phrases, and even whole sentences that we men know nothing about. There are even facial expressions in this language which are totally lost on men.

It's uncanny how a bunch of women and girls can sit around a table and give each other knowing looks when some man does or says something dumb. They don't even have to know one another, and they don't need to say a word. They just know.

Women and girls have lots of skills and abilities that we men don't have. For example, both my wife and my daughter can each read a text message out loud and express the exact intended tone and attitude of the person who sent it. I listen in amazement as they do this.

Text messages always just look like words on a screen to me. How they know that the sender, usually a guy, was injecting love, sarcasm, apathy, or other emotions into those typed words on a phone is beyond me.

It is fascinating to watch them analyze and read out loud a text message from a young man my daughter is dating. I'm like, "How do you know to read that one sweetly?"

They are best at reading groveling apologies out loud. They both can sure make a guy sound sorry.

Women and girls seem to enjoy analyzing a few short text messages for hours. I've often thought there should be an app for that.

But I digress. Back to their special language. A case in point is the phrase "Is he rehabilitatable?" I'm not sure the big word in that sentence is even a real word. I've never heard this phrase used outside of a prison context, or in the context I am about to describe.

When I was single in the early 1980s, I asked my now-wife out on a date. I considered myself to be a very snappy dresser in 1982, although I found out later that my clothes then had been snappy back in 1974.

For our first date, I put on my sexy Pierre Cardin crimson red short-sleeve shirt, my best pair of black polyester bell bottom slacks, my black Beatles shoes, and an Argentinian camel colored leather jacket that I bought in Providence, Rhode Island.

I splashed on some Brut cologne and unbuttoned the top two buttons in my shirt to show off my gold chain and St. Christopher's medal. (This worked for Travolta).

I slipped into my matching gold 1972 Mercury Marquis Brougham, which got seven miles to a gallon of gas, and ten miles to a quart of oil. Off I went, windows down, to pick up my date.

Ellen met me at the door of her apartment. Her eyes widened as she took in my outfit. I could tell she was impressed, even though she didn't say anything at all about my wardrobe. Just think when she checks out my wheels, I thought! As we got down to the street, I could tell she was the athletic type, because she just kept walking right past my car, even as I opened the passenger side door. I guess she wanted to walk to the restaurant. Once we got to the restaurant, which was only five miles away, she put on her sunglasses as we enjoyed our meal and great conversation. I loved that movie star look. It was a terrific date, but I was really tired from all that walking. I don't kiss and tell, but I can tell you we had a second date.

I decided to go for broke on our second date, and I wore my best leisure suit. I thought we were going to go to a movie, but when I picked her up this time, I found out how generous she was. She took me to the mall instead, and we went clothes shopping, for me! And did we ever shop. Ellen picked out all sorts of shirts, slacks, jackets, and sweaters.

"This will look great on you," she'd say. Or, "I think

you should try these slacks with this jacket." She even tried to pay for some of the purchases, but I wasn't having any of that!

I could tell she was falling for me, but I found it peculiar that she asked me to leave my favorite beige faux leather leisure suit in the dressing room. Oh well, I could come back for it later, but later never came.

Even though I had all these new clothes, old habits die hard. So, on our third date, I wore my light blue plaid sport coat and best purple tie. Off to the mall we went again. My date really liked to shop! Once again, my sport coat and favorite tie disappeared in the changing room.

Alas, it was only after we had been married a few years that I learned the cold, hard truth. On each of those first few dates, my future wife was contemplating but a single thought, a question that had been pondered and shared by single women everywhere for millennia: "Is he rehabilitatable?"

And this wasn't just a private thought. Oh no, she had lengthy serious discussions on the subject, both by phone and in person, with her mother.

"Do you think he might ask you to marry him?"

"I think he might, Mom."

"What about the clothes?"

"I know, right!"

"Well?"

"Do you mean, 'Is he rehabilitatable?'"

"Of course that's what I mean."

I learned later that all women, everywhere, ponder this very same question when they see a dating couple out in public.

It's not just clothes either. When we were about to get married and were combining households, I parked a truck with all my earthly bachelor possessions at her house.

"Just leave that moving van in the driveway for now," my bride-to-be said. "I have some friends who will help us move your stuff later."

I loved her and trusted her with all my heart, of course, but I would really like to know what happened to my oscilloscope—the one that I had always kept on my dining room table, and the yellow PVC lawn furniture from my living room when I was a bachelor.

It took several years for me to learn that rehabilitation comes in stages for married men. First, there is the list of clothes, and colors, and patterns that we are NOT allowed to buy, or wear, ever. Plaid sports coats, purple ties, and leisure suits are now forever off limits for me. If we prove ourselves trustworthy, then we are allowed to dress ourselves in the morning, as long as the shirt we are going to wear is on the same hanger as the suitcoat, and the tie is there too. It's sort of like going to a diner with a policy of "No substitutions allowed!"

Ellen and I got married in my first semester of law school. I've come a long way since then. Now I can buy my own shirts, as long as they come from Brooks Brothers, and are in a preapproved color, i.e., one I've bought before. Every day, before I leave for work, I ask her, "Do I look like a lawyer?"

She just smiles. I've been rehabilitated.

Destiny

Have you ever paused and taken a snapshot of your life, and all the people in it, and wondered how it came to be that you are where you are? What brought you and all these people into your life at this point in time? Did you zig when you could have zagged, said yes instead of no, turned right instead of left? Did you take a chance when you didn't have to? Did they all do the same? Was it destiny?

Did you ever wonder if your life would be different now if you'd hit the game-winning home run in the bottom of the ninth inning with two outs way back when, or if you had correctly spelled that impossible word in the last round of the school spelling bee?

Destiny is a complex thing. Every step you take, every person you meet, every decision you make—all these things affect everything else that follows. Turn right and your life follows one path, turn left and it follows another. Say yes and the world is your oyster, say no and you land in the gutter.

I once dated a girl named Sally who aspired to marry a doctor. She let me down easy when she learned that I didn't own a stethoscope. We remained close friends. Some years later, I received an invitation to the wedding of Sally and Dr. Ed.

A peculiar note was written on the invitation in Sally's neat cursive. "Dear Bob, Come alone, do NOT bring a date. Love, Sally. P.S.—I'm going to fix you up with someone!"

I called Sally right away.

"Sally," I said, "Let me get this straight. You want me to come to your wedding ALONE? There will be 250 people at your reception. I will be seated at a table of nine because I will be the only person without a date."

"Everyone will ask what everyone asks at weddings: 'How do you know the bride and groom?' "I dated the bride, but she dumped me to marry him!" will be my response.

"Trust me, Bob. I'm going to introduce you to someone."

Should I trust her? Should I go? Should I zig, or should I zag?

I did what I always do when facing a big decision. I took a slow stroll around Goat Island, where the rushing waters calm your soul and clarify your thoughts, where the thunder of Niagara makes your heart beat its way to the truth. Something in the river air told me I should take a chance.

I went to the church alone. It was a beautiful ceremony. As I took my seat, I noticed the most beautiful woman I had ever seen. She was sitting in the pew in front of me.

She was there with her parents. No escort. No ring on her left hand.

I have to meet her, I thought. But woe is me. Sally is going to fix me up with someone else.

I found my seat at the reception at a table set for ten. There were four couples and me. I was next to an adjacent empty chair. I explained to the woman to my left how I knew the bride, where we had gone on our dates, and why I hadn't gone to medical school.

She offered "I'm sorry" sentiments from time to time as I scanned the room for the beautiful woman I had seen in the church.

As dinner ended, the bride and groom rose from the head table and started to make the rounds to greet their guests. Sally spotted me from afar and detoured to another table. She took the hand of her fixer-upper candidate and started toward my table. I squinted hard as they made their approach.

Could it be? Yes! Sally was guiding the most beautiful woman straight toward me!

"Bob, I'd like you to meet Ellen. Ellen, this is my friend Bob, who is not a doctor. You two should go get married."

And we did, eventually.

But not before Ellen's twelve-year-old brother Michael sat down next to us at our table and cross-examined me. The questions came like rapid-fire:

"What kind of car do you drive?"

"What is your occupation?"

"Are you a Republican or Democrat?"

"What is your religion?"

"Do you go to church?"

"What is your annual income?"

"Where do you see yourself in ten years?"

The inquisition continued until dessert was served. Her brother was so busy playing Perry Mason that he dipped his spoon into a dish full of butter, mistaking it for ice cream. I watched as he brought the spoonful to his mouth.

Should I tell him?

Nah! I suppressed my smile as he rushed off to the restroom.

I asked Ellen to dance as Gordon Lightfoot sang "Beautiful." Gordon was right. I couldn't have agreed more. I couldn't have imagined how Ellen could have been anything but beautiful to me. We danced the night away.

Conversation was easy. It was as if we had known each other our whole lives. This was destiny, I thought.

It wasn't long before I found myself strolling around Goat Island, contemplating whether I should ask Ellen to marry me. It was a very short stroll.

She said yes!

We had a September wedding at the very same church where I had first laid eyes on the most beautiful woman I had ever seen.

Sally and Ed smiled from their pew as we said our vows. Sally blew us a kiss as we walked down the center aisle as husband and wife.

Ellen and I danced to "Beautiful" as our first dance as husband and wife. We spent our wedding night at the Prince of Wales Hotel at Niagara-on-the-Lake. We walked along the Niagara River the next morning and talked about our future. Love was in the air. That's what Niagara is all about.

I didn't hit the game-winning home run. I didn't spell the impossible word. And I didn't take the easy way out.

I zigged when I could have zagged.

I took a stroll around Goat Island and decided to take a chance and go to a wedding where the only person I knew was the bride. It was there that I met the most beautiful woman I've ever known, my best friend, the love of my life, my wife.

The moral of my story is this: If someone you used to date invites you to their wedding, and that person is not marrying you, you should go to the wedding anyway.

Give destiny a chance.

Dahlia Bulbs and Sauce

I grew up in the city of Niagara Falls. We had DiCamillo's Bakery, Trusello's Pizza, and the Como Restaurant. We had salt and crushed red pepper shakers on our kitchen tables. We had ravioli for lunch, linguini for dinner, and biscotti for dessert.

I learned the seven vowels of the alphabet from my elementary school friends. They had names like Carella, DeLuca, DelMonte, DiGregorio, Fabiano, Fasciano, Mariani, Nardelli, Nicolette, and Vicino. My football coach was Calandrelli, a beautiful name that flows off your tongue like sauce on capellini.

In my Boy Scout troop, we joked that you could get a merit badge in Italian if you could spell Castiglione, and become an Eagle Scout if you could pronounce Pasqualichio.

Most of my friends were Italian, and the rest wanted to be. Maybe New York had Little Italy, but we had the entire island of Sicily on Pine Avenue. I grew a moustache at age fourteen, partly so I could buy beer at the delicatessen at 22nd Street and Grand Avenue, but mostly because I wanted to look Italian. Who would ask a 14-year-old with a moustache for proof of age, right? I still sport that moustache today.

I married into an Italian family.

"I'm Italian," I told my bride. "I'm from Niagara Falls. Look. I've got a moustache!"

"Prove it!" she said. "Make me some sauce."

My dad was a good cook. He wasn't Italian, but I asked him for advice. He grew his own basil and garlic in our backyard. Basil is a cash crop in Niagara Falls. He gave me some garlic bulbs. "Plant these."

I had never tried to grow something you could eat. I had only ever planted flowers.

I waited months for that garlic to grow. Pressure mounted. My bride wanted sauce. I couldn't wait any longer.

I dug up the bulbs and sautéed them with pork and Italian sausage. I simmered that sauce for hours. I made some spaghetti from scratch.

Francis Bacon once said: "Man prefers to believe what he prefers to be true." I preferred to believe I was Italian and could make sauce. I ladled my creation over the spaghetti.

My bride twirled a few strands of sauce-covered spaghetti around her fork. She added a bulb to the forkful and took a bite.

She delicately removed the bulb from her mouth. She placed the bulb on her plate and studied it. She raised it to her nose and took a sniff. Then she burst out laughing.

"I'm calling your mother!" she exclaimed.

I have good news and bad news. The good news is that dahlia bulbs are not poisonous. The bad news is that dahlia bulbs are flavorless, and I'm apparently not Italian.

Wine Tastings and the Law School Admission Test

I had three inventions to my name by late summer of 1983. I had invented the first, an electric yo-yo, for a speech in Mr. Welch's English Class at Gaskill Junior High. The neat thing about that invention was that it went up and down by itself, freeing your hands to do other things. I sold about 30 of them to my teachers and classmates for $3.95 each. The teachers paid cash; my classmates gave me 300 Bazooka Bubble Gum wrappers.

Mr. Welch gave me an A+ for the speech. He told me that he had never seen students stay past the afternoon closing bell to listen to a story. He encouraged me to keep inventing, and to start thinking about law school.

My next invention was in high school. I invented and built the world's first digital chess clock for the Niagara Falls High School Chess Club, but couldn't afford to patent it.

My third invention came from a restaurant experience. I always enjoyed a cup of coffee after dinner, but I was sensitive to caffeine, so I always asked for decaf. The server has the choice of a green or orange carafe, and you don't find out until you've paid the bill, tipped the server, and are wired at 3 a.m. that you didn't get decaf—you got high-test.

So I invented the caffeine test strip. You dip it in your coffee cup at a restaurant. If the strip turned orange, it was caffeinated; if the strip turned green, it was decaf; if the strip turned pink, you were pregnant. My heart was broken when I found the test strips had been invented first by somebody else, sans the pregnancy test, and you could buy them for $5.95 a box.

This inventing caused me to develop an aching desire to go to law school and become a patent lawyer. My fiancée, Ellen, encouraged me to pursue my dream, and promised to support me if I did. I was living in Kentucky, and I called the local law school to inquire about their evening program. I told them my college GPA, and asked them what I needed to score on the law school admission test (LSAT) to gain admittance.

The admissions officer just laughed. "Sir," she said, "with grades like yours, all you have to do is take the LSAT exam and you will be admitted!"

I took her at her word, and went to a wine tasting the evening before the LSAT, an error in judgment on my part. Surprisingly, I don't remember the wine tasting in detail, but I do remember that there were thirteen bottles: six whites, six reds, and one champagne. I developed a fondness for *pinot noir* that night.

The next morning, I literally slept through the first 30 minutes of the LSAT. It was the first time in my life I actually scored a zero on part of an exam. My younger brother, who had many such experiences, tried to console me. I scored on the 69th percentile of all test takers. It made me feel proud at the time that I was pretty smart even while asleep. My wife later explained to me that only a single guy could have been so stupid.

But, no worries, I was admitted to law school, and was off to the races.

Mark Twain once said that he "joined the Confederacy, served for two weeks, deserted and the Confederacy fell." Well I stayed in the night law school program for two weeks, just enough time to know I loved it, and then deserted. Unlike the Confederacy, the law school flourished after I left.

I applied to the State University at Buffalo Law School for the next year, but my combined GPA and LSAT scores just weren't high enough for admittance. I was waitlisted.

Day after day, week after week, month after month, I waited. I rewrote my essay. I tried to explain how *pinot noir* affected my LSAT score, but to no avail. Orientation was on Monday, August 20, 1984. On Friday, August 17, I was still not admitted. My phone rang.

Ellen told me that her mom had an idea. "My mom thinks you should drive from Cincinnati to Buffalo, show up at orientation, and see if someone didn't show up!"

"Is your mom crazy? They don't want me! I'm not smart enough. Let's try again next year," I said.

"What do you have to lose?" Ellen asked.

Then she uttered those five magical words no guy in love can refuse: "Please do it for me!"

So I got into my Camaro and drove to Buffalo.

I put on my best gray suit on Monday morning and went to the dean's office. I had no appointment. There were 284 first-year law students gathered for orientation when I introduced myself to the dean's secretary, told her I was on the wait list, had driven six hours from Cincinnati, and wondered if the dean might give me five minutes of his time. I could tell she had never heard such a thing before.

"Please have a seat," she said before entering the dean's private office.

To my great surprise, the dean came out of his office to greet me. He asked how he could help me.

"I'm on the wait list," I told him. "I want to come to this law school, and I want to be a lawyer. I drove six hours to come to orientation just to ask you if there is anyone who was admitted who didn't show up for orientation? Might you have room for one more student?"

"Why do you want to be a lawyer?" he asked.

"I want to help people patent their inventions. I want to help people in general, and I want to learn my craft at this law school," I told him.

I added, "If you don't admit me this year, I will return, year after year, until you do!"

He shook my hand, told me to go to orientation that day and come back to see him the next day at 2 p.m.

I hardly slept that night. I went to orientation the next morning. All the other students had an "orientation packet." I felt like they were all looking at me and wondering why I didn't have a packet. I was the only one in the room wearing a suit.

At 2 p.m., I went back to the dean's office. The secretary asked me to take a seat. The dean was behind two French doors in a conference room meeting with the admissions committee. The room was right in front of me. I shook in my boots for fifteen minutes staring at those closed doors. It seemed like an eternity.

Finally the French doors opened. I could see a long conference room table. There were five law professors on one side of the table, and five on the other. The Dean was at the head of the table, facing me. All of these professors of law turned their heads in unison and looked at me. They looked grim and serious. I prepared for the worst.

The dean stood up, walked around the table and approached me. I rose to greet him. He had a grim, serious look on his face. Then he stopped, extended his hand, and smiled. "Congratulations, Bob, you are the 285th and final student admitted to the UB Law School Class of 1987. Go buy your books!" The law professors broke into applause. I peeked around the dean and saw them smiling at me. I thanked the dean profusely and shook his hand with both of mine.

I ran from his office and found a phone booth on the first floor of the school. I called Ellen and told her the news. We were ecstatic. We got married the next month. I sat in the last row of every class that first year. I am probably the only student in the history of the law school to know that I was the last person admitted to my class. I went through the whole first year thinking, "He is smarter than me, she is smarter than me." In a way, they were. I'm pretty sure none of them went to a wine tasting the day before the LSAT.

There's a famous line in *The Princess Bride*: "Never cross a Sicilian when death is on the line." My mother-in-law is Sicilian. I prefer, "Always trust a Sicilian when law school is on the line." I will always be indebted to her for asking Ellen to make that call.

In my second year of law school, the dean decided to teach a course on intellectual property law. He asked me if I would teach the section on patent law to the class. After that day, I stopped sitting in the last row. It meant so much that he trusted me. I've been teaching patent law at the law school for thirteen years now. It's my way of giving back. I tell this story every year to my students. My hope is that I inspire some student who might feel like I did way back when, that he or she isn't quite smart enough to be there.

Marriage and the Lottery

It was a beautiful Sunday morning during our first year of marriage. My new wife was reading the Sunday paper. I held a lottery ticket in my hand.

"Would you find the winning lottery numbers and read them to me out loud?" I asked.

"Sure," she said. She found the lottery page and looked up to see if I was ready.

"2," she said.

"Uh-huh," I replied.

"16."

"Yep."

"24."

"Got it."

With each number she read she looked up innocently as if she thought we were on our way to striking gold.

I didn't disappoint. I stared at the ticket intently with each number she announced. My eyes widened with each number. The excitement grew. I let her think we were hitting each number, but the truth is none of the numbers she read were on my ticket.

By the fourth number, my guilt was beginning to build in parallel with her excitement. The happiness I'd been feeling at my clever prank diminished as my guilt grew. I was lucky enough to have married someone who trusted me so completely that she actually believed I was being truthful.

How could I be so mean to this beautiful wife of mine? How could I string her along so mercilessly? What kind of a person was I?

After all, she was a certified public accountant. She was an order of magnitude smarter than me. I never thought my silly prank would get this far.

But there we were.

I was ready to confess after the third number, then the fourth, but I didn't quite know how. By the fifth

number, there was no turning back. I was completely caught in a web of lottery deceit.

She caught on about two seconds after announcing the sixth number.

"Bob!" she sputtered as she threw the whole Sunday paper at me. It was a good thing she didn't have something heavier or sharper to throw. And it was a very good thing that I had found and married a woman who was not only beautiful but who had a good sense of humor.

Last Sunday morning—in our 34th year of marriage—I held a lottery ticket in my hand. My wife was reading the Sunday morning paper.

"Would you mind reading me the winning lottery numbers?" I asked.

She smiled sweetly and handed me the paper. "Read your own damn numbers."

She's been saying the same thing every Sunday morning for 33 years.

I won the lottery when she married me!

Store Returns

The Guinness World Record people called me the other day. They took me totally by surprise. It turns out that, of the 7.5 billion people on the earth, and all the people who have ever purchased anything at a brick and mortar or online store, I am now tied with a fellow named Amadi from Ethiopia for returning the fewest purchased items to a store. That's right! Amadi and I have each returned only one item we purchased to a store in all our days of shopping. Amadi returned a dromedary camel one day – its hump was "too small."

It's not that I don't shop. I do. I buy all sorts of things. OK, actually I don't. I mostly buy electronic gadgets, chess books, chess sets and socks. Sometimes I buy shoes too. The Best Buy greeter actually greets me with "Hi Bob!" Sometimes on the weekend I hang out with the greeter and help him direct customers to specific departments. If I'm not busy I'll help them sell some cameras or explain the signal to noise ratios on their sound systems to customers.

Actually, part of the reason for my prudent shopping record is that I only shop at five brick and mortar stores: Best Buy, Ed Young's Hardware, Riverside Men's Shop, Wegmans, and Home Depot. I have never set foot in a Walmart or Target. I buy all my shoes from Allen Edmonds in Port Washington, Wisconsin, and all my shirts from Brooks Brothers. Everything else I buy from Amazon, and Alexa helps me with that.

Amazingly, in all my days on earth, and all my days inside retail stores, and with all the items I've added to my shopping cart, I've only returned a single, solitary item to a store, and that was back in 1984. More about that later.

It's not that I have never made a buying mistake. Maybe I have. I just won't admit it. I sometimes stand with my cart and admire people in line at the "service desk" returning items they purchased in error. I strain to hear what they are saying: "It doesn't fit." "It doesn't work." "It's purple." And so on. I've never heard one of these people admit, "I made a mistake. I bought the wrong thing! I'm stupid." Sometimes I privately question their honesty.

I've tried on occasion to muster the courage to return things to a store. There were a whole bunch of Black and Decker power tools my wife wouldn't let me play with when we remodeled our house, for example. There was that ugly Christmas sweater my brother gave me one year, and, of course, those black polyester bell bottoms I had bought in 1995. I've gone so far as to drive to the store, put the items in a cart, and walk toward the pneumatic door. Once I even entered the store, but chickened out and did a u-turn back to my car. All these items are neatly arranged on shelves in an auxiliary "possible store returns" room adjacent my man-cave. It is sort of like a museum of my life shopping adventures.

This is definitely not a genetic trait. My wife and daughter have mastered the art of store returns. They visit the UPS store at least twice a week. Every Thursday when I take the trash bins to the end of the driveway my wife warns me, "Not that dear. That's a store return!" My wife has a macro in Microsoft Word for completing product return forms. She and my daughter call them PRFs to save time.

My wife is also a master at preserving "original packaging." Not me. When I unpackaged my new Wi-Fi enabled Philips Hue White and Color Ambiance Beyond Dimmable Smart Table Lamp with two independent uplight and downlight sources, the box it came in was unrecognizable and Styrofoam particles floated through the air for days like puffballs of white fuzz on a blooming dandelion. What is it about Styrofoam anyway? It's magnetic! No matter how hard you shake your fingers you can't get if off your body once it finds you!

Getting back to my world record, I thank my teachers for that. They taught me that mistakes are bad. They keep you from getting a gold star on your homework paper and from getting tickets to ride the roller coaster at Crystal Beach from Tops Market for your report card. So I've become the world's most efficient shopper, along with my friend Amadi from Ethiopia. I've never made a buying mistake in my life that I will admit to. I decide what I want and sometimes I even buy what I need. Once the cash leaves my hand or the card is swiped, that's it! There is no going back.

Well, except that one time, when it happened …

It was 1984. I was a newly-wed. I didn't know the rules of marriage. We had a television stand. We had a television. There was an extra shelf on the stand. I was unemployed. I was a law student. I bought a VCR from Kmart for $350 on Tuesday. I surprised my wife when she got home from work that evening. I was so proud to show her that I had programmed it so the display stopped blinking. We returned it to the store on Wednesday. She drove me. She watched me as I carried it to the service desk. The lady asked me the reason for the return.

"I'm a newlywed." She just smiled and nodded. I have never set foot in a Kmart since.

Bingo or Chess?

There is nothing quite like the game of bingo to demonstrate the superiority of the female mind. My wife sometimes goes with her mom to play at St. Amelia's Church in Tonawanda.

"Why don't you come along?" they ask.

"No thanks," I would respond politely. "I prefer the intellectual challenge of chess."

I had no interest in bingo. Besides, they played on the same day my chess club met.

Ellen smiled coyly when I declined her invitation. She smiled in that special way a wife smiles when she knows something that her husband doesn't.

And then it happened...

My Wednesday chess club meeting was cancelled. It was the 45th anniversary of the Fischer-Spassky World Chess Championship, and all my friends were staying home to watch a documentary on the event.

Ellen sympathized with my disappointment. "Why don't you come to St. Amelia's with us for a fun night of daubing?" she asked.

I didn't really want to go. But I had been an altar boy as a kid and St. Amelia's needed the money. I went with them for the good of the church.

It was a mind-numbing experience. There were 1,000 people packed into the church hall, each heavily armed with bingo supplies. I didn't even know there were bingo supplies. There was pizza and donuts and soft drinks and coffee. There were score boards like in a football stadium. There were numbered ping-pong balls bouncing around like popcorn in a big fish aquarium.

A Grand Knight of the Knights of Columbus was behind a microphone booming letters and numbers into the public address system. There was excitement in the air such as I have rarely known. I couldn't wait to describe this spectacle to my chess buddies.

We lined up to buy cards. My wife and mother-in-law bought nine cards each for every game.

I handed the bingo card lady a large bill. "I'll take twenty cards," I said with the confidence of a chess player.

"Give him six cards," my wife said.

"Better make that four," her mother said.

Oh, they of little faith.

My wife and her mother made a beeline for a table and we took our seats. My wife was on my left and my mother-in-law was on my right. I was in the middle so they could keep an eye on me and my cards.

"Line your cards up like this," my wife said. She had her nine cards arranged in three rows of three. Her mom did the same. I laid out my four lonely cards in an embarrassing two-by-two square.

My wife gave me a package of bingo daubers. I spent most of the evening trying to use the word "daub" in a sentence. Then I just started playing with the daubers. I was daubing everything I could—my bingo card, my forearm, a hot dog, a piece of pizza, and the forehead of a sweet old lady sitting across from me. I gave her the measles with my red dauber. I spent the first fifteen minutes figuring out which color dauber to use. There were so many choices!

Then I devised a daubing system. I would use red for even numbers, blue for odd numbers, and I would show them what a chess player could do with a simple game like bingo. I even decided I would daub with both hands!

Well, I got so distracted by the daubers that I didn't notice the Grand Knight starting to announce numbers into the microphone. The whole hall quieted down. His voice was somehow soothing and melodic. I shifted my focus to the unending sequence of combinations—of three consonants, two vowels, and a number between 1 and 75.

"B-13, G-55, O-70..."

It was oddly comforting, kind of like a performance

of chamber music in an 18th century Vienna concert hall. I was lulled into calculating the number of possible combinations of letters and numbers on all the cards in the church hall that night. Accounting for the free space, it turns out that there are 552,446,474,061,128,648,601,600,000, or approximately 5.52×10^{26} combinations.

While deep in calculation, I was suddenly jolted back to the game by a flurry of hands and daubers flying in front of my face from my right and my left. Blue, green, pink, yellow, and red daubers, all the colors of the rainbow, flying in like jet planes with pinpoint accuracy to daub my cards. It was a thing of beauty to behold, like robotic arms in an automobile assembly line.

They so impressed me as they daubed not only their own nine cards, but all four of mine, at the same time! And they didn't just mark the last number announced. They went back in time to the beginning! They could remember like a dozen numbers. All this time I was searching all my cards for "B-15." I couldn't find it anywhere. Sensing my frustration, my elderly friend with the measles gently whispered, "Top left card, dear, first column, two numbers from the top!" How she knew I was looking for that number, and found it while reading my cards upside down, while tracking nine cards of her own, is just a really big bingo mystery. I would not want to play chess against that lady!

By the third game of the evening, I was really starting to get the hang of it. I was daubing like a veteran. I was holding pizza in my left hand, sipping a Coke through a straw, and daubing with my right hand at the same time.

I was "on the bubble" when the hallucination hit me square between the eyes. Could it be? Yes!

"Bingo!" I called with the confidence of a chess player delivering checkmate.

Sighs of disappointment murmured through the hall. My wife and mother-in-law looked over my cards.

They looked up in tandem, each wearing an expression that seemed to say, "We are really sorry for the embarrassment you are about to experience."

I had mis-daubed. I didn't even know that was a word.

"He was just practicing!" my wife said apologetically to the Grand Knight.

The Grand Knight started to announce numbers again. The excitement started to build again. No one seemed to notice as I excused myself and headed for the restroom. I called an Uber and headed home.

I dreamt that night about fianchettoing my bishop in the Sicilian Defense. I would never play bingo again. That game was just too damn hard!

Tax Law, True Love, and the Socratic Method

If you are not familiar with the Socratic Method, take a look at the 1973 movie, *The Paper Chase*, and watch Professor Kingsfield drill unprepared first year law student James Hart on a contract case in full view of his classmates. Hart squirms and sweats and becomes so upset and humiliated that he throws up in the bathroom after class.

By the time I went to law school in the 80s, most of my professors had thankfully abandoned the Socratic Method while other kind teachers had softened the approach. Such was not the case with Professor Bennett in Federal Tax Law 101, a required course in the fall semester of 1985. Professor Bennett was a dynamo and fountain of tax law information. We students privately referred to her as Professor Internal Revenue. She knew her stuff and expected all of us to know it too.

There were 142 students crowded into Room 106 of

O'Brian Hall every Monday and Wednesday at 8 a.m. It is safe to say most of us didn't want to be there. First, it was tax law, and, second, it was 8 o'clock in the morning. Maybe it's just me, but I don't think any course, on any subject, should be taught at 8 a.m., EVER! Besides, I had a very personal and private reason for not wanting to take this course.

When single and dating, and way before eHarmony.com, I had my own prioritized wish list and algorithms for dating and trying to find the woman I would hope to marry. First, she would be sweet and kind. Second, she would be smart. Third, she would occasionally laugh at my jokes. Last, but not least, she would be a Certified Public Accountant, on account of some embarrassing overdraft notices I was regularly receiving from my bank.

It was surprisingly difficult to find someone who met my short list of requirements. For example, I once dated a very sweet, very smart lumberjack who laughed at all my jokes. But she couldn't even fill out a 1040 short form!

I hit the jackpot when I met Ellen. She is sweet, kind, smart, gorgeous, a CPA, and she laughed at all, then most, and then some of my jokes for the first few years of our marriage. In our wedding vows, I promised to love, honor, obey, and entertain. She promised to love, honor, pick out my clothes for work, and do our tax returns.

I was very busy in that fall of '85. I was taking five courses, writing for the Law Review, competing in moot court, clerking at a law firm, and working on my stamp collection. I had no time for tax law. I had no need for tax law.

On my way to class every morning, I muttered the same phrase over and over. "I married a CPA. She doesn't let me touch the checkbook. Why do I need to know tax law?"

I was so busy that I fell behind in my reading. But my sweet wife came to the rescue. She loved tax law! She read my tax law case book just for fun! We made a deal. She wouldn't make fun of me for collecting stamps, and I wouldn't make fun of her for reading tax law cases just for fun.

Ellen agreed to read and brief all the tax cases for me. This is one of those deep personal marital secrets that should probably never be exposed, but every Monday and Wednesday morning, between 7 and 7:15 a.m. in September, October, and November of 1985, as I was standing over a sink shaving and brushing my teeth, my beautiful, smart wife would brief me on three tax cases assigned for my 8 a.m. class. How lucky can a guy possibly be?

And then it happened ...

On a crisp October morning, I took my usual seat in the back row of Room 106. I had escaped Professor Bennett's attention for a month and a half. I was halfway home. I wasn't worried. I had a bundle of Ellen's briefs. I was prepared.

Professor Bennett perused her seating chart. She

looked up from her chart and surveyed the rows of students. She was looking for her next victim. Then she started off class that day with a booming, "Mr. Simpson!"

She locked her sights on me from across the classroom as my 141 classmates breathed a collective sigh of relief. The overhead lights dimmed and the spotlight shown on me alone. Heads turned as my classmates in the rows ahead settled in for the interrogation. All 284 eyeballs focused like lasers on me.

"Stevens versus the IRS," continued Professor Bennett. "Please enlighten us on the facts of the case, Mr. Simpson."

I discreetly pulled out Ellen's case brief about a case I never read, and managed to recite the facts as if I had written the opinion myself!

The professor seemed unimpressed. "Please explain the holding, the rule of law, and the takeaway from this case."

I continued to expound on a case I knew nothing about, impressing myself. I had won. I would not be throwing up in the bathroom after this class!

But, no! She wasn't through. "Funk v. Wagnalls, Mr. Simpson. Tell us about that case if you please."

"So that's how it's going to be," I murmured under my breath as I scanned Ellen's notes. "OK, it's time to show off." I proceeded to tell the good professor and all of my classmates everything they would ever want to know about that case, and then some. I even ad-libbed about depreciation and travel expenses. I was talking about debits and credits when she cut me off. I had nailed it!

Then she did the unthinkable! Never before in O'Brian Hall had a professor drilled one student about three consecutive cases in a single setting. But there she was, standing in the front of the vast lecture hall, her eyes still locked on me. "Smith v. Wesson," she said. "What about Smith v. Wesson?"

I gave her the facts perfectly, then the holding, then the rule of law, and then the takeaway. I was playing poker with four aces up my sleeve. I was so full of myself I was about to explode!

Then she asked me the question no law student ever wants to hear. "What about the dissent?"

I looked down at Ellen's cheat sheet and found the heading "Dissent." But THE SPACE BELOW THE HEADING WAS BLANK! Nothing. Nada. What to do!

The spotlight grew brighter as sweat beaded on my forehead. I had come so far, only to be sunk by a dissenting opinion. I hadn't read the dissent in this or any other case. None of my friends ever read the dissents either. We were too busy reading majority opinions to read opinions by judges who didn't get their way. It wasn't the law anyway.

I decided to come clean.

"I don't know what the dissent said," I boldly proclaimed, as my professor smiled like a spider who had just caught a fly in her web. She could have ended it there, but no.

"Why DON'T you know what the dissent said?" she inquired.

282 eyes turned in my direction, as I fabricated my best lie. "I read the dissent three weeks ago when the case was first assigned, but since we have fallen behind schedule on the syllabus, I just forgot what the dissent said."

My classmates turned back to her.

"Is THAT what you are going to tell your tax clients who come to see you, Mr. Simpson? That you don't remember the case because you read it a few weeks ago?"

141 heads turned back my way, just like an old commercial. "When E.F. Hutton talks, people listen."

"No." I kept my reply short and simple, hoping she would move on.

"What WILL you tell that tax client?"

I could feel the noose tighten. I paused, reflected, pondered, looked for escape routes, and then decided to end these head-turning calisthenics once and for all.

"Well professor," I explained. "First, I will ask that tax client why they are coming to see a registered patent attorney for TAX advice! THEN, I will refer that client to you, but ONLY if you move on quickly to another case and another student!"

I had immediate doubts about that remark, but Professer Bennett actually smiled. Then came spontaneous applause and laughter from my classmates.

Professor Bennett moved on to the next case and another student.

Three years after my graduation from law school my phone rang. It was a prospective patent client, one I would go on to do a lot of work for. One day I asked him how he found me. It turned out he'd been referred by a law school classmate whom I had never met and didn't know.

I called my classmate on the phone to thank him and asked him if we ever met.

"We've never spoken," he said. "But I sat two rows ahead of you in Tax Law. The only thing I remember about that class was when you asked why a client with tax law issues would seek advice from a patent attorney."

I've taught patent law at the law school now for many years. I always encourage my students to speak up in class. I limit my "interrogations" to two cases per student. And I never ask my students about dissenting opinions.

P.S. Dianne Bennett is a brilliant lawyer and was one of my favorite professors. I received my law degree in 1987, without ever having read a tax case. I received an honors grade from her. I haven't reviewed a bank statement since 1984. Ellen received her law degree, magna cum laude, *in 1990. She asks me to sign a 1040 tax return every April 15. I still collect stamps, and she still reads tax law opinions just for fun.*

A Day at Niagara with a Phony Tour Guide

If you are a native of Niagara Falls like me, and if you sometimes host guests and visitors from out of town and give them tours, then surely you know that they expect you to know every single fact about the Falls. Why is it that visitors always assume that natives know everything about their hometowns? We get used to the usual questions here: How high are the American Falls? (176 feet) How high are the Horseshoe Falls? (167 feet) Are Canadians taller than Americans? (No, but they are better skaters, eh!) True natives know how deep the Niagara River is (170 feet) and how Goat Island got its name (because an early settler, John Stedman, had few friends and lots of goats and rowed them there to protect them from wolves.)

Eventually—and this happens to all of us, we get asked a question we don't know the answer to. This can be quite embarrassing and downright upsetting if you are not prepared for it. This happened to me last summer when a friend and his mom were visiting from Argentina and I offered to show them around. We started with the Lockport locks (which I knew little about) and the story of the Erie Canal. The questions from my guests were coming so fast and furious that I excused myself to use the restroom, bought a few books from the gift shop *en route*, and emerged an expert on Irish canal construction.

It used to bother me that I didn't know all the answers to these questions when playing tour guide. I would stay up late the night before the tour, studying up on local history. They don't teach us this stuff in school, after all, and I didn't learn it at home either. To me, Goat Island was just a cool place to ride my bike, and Prospect Point was where we went to cool off on a hot summer day. But the more tours I gave, and the more questions I was asked that I didn't have answers for, the more uncomfortable I became. I even considered retiring from the tour guide business altogether.

And then it happened...

One day, quite by accident, as I was leading a group of overly inquisitive out-of-town friends around Goat Island, they started asking me all sorts of questions:

"What kind of butterfly was that?" asked Joe.

"A Monarch," I replied as I described a moth.

"What kind of tree is that?" asked Sally.

"A Sequoia," I responded to describe a maple.

"And that bird?" asked Tom.

"Oh, that's an ostrich," I said as I described a seagull.

With each lie I told, my confidence grew. It turns out that the faster you answer a question, the more likely the person who asked it will believe you. Every answer I gave was instantly accepted as truth, as long as I spit it out a few seconds after the query was received. In no time at all, lies were gushing from my mouth like water flowing over the brink!

Before long I wasn't just lying, I was making up whole stories. I can't tell you how many times I personally went over the Falls in barrels, inner tubes, and refrigerators in these stories. I even went over standing on a surfboard dressed like Superman while waving to my friends on the bank. It's all about looking your guests straight in the eye and lying with all your heart.

As your powers of embellishment develop, you can have a lot of fun giving tours around the Falls. Oh sure, you can't fool everyone. Canadians are off limits, and so are the Japanese. They just laugh at you and tell you that you are lying. But I've had exceptional success with Americans who didn't grow up here.

My absolute favorite thing to do is this. As every

Niagarian knows, all guests on the Maid of the Mist boat tour are given blue rain ponchos to wear. You can use this fact to your advantage if you are an embellisher like me.

We've all been there—taking someone on that joyful ride for the first time—experiencing the majesty of Niagara through the eyes of a newbie. And we've all seen the simultaneous fear and wonderment in those eyes. It doesn't matter that the captain explains that the boat has three 500 horsepower engines, and that only one is needed to turn around and not get sucked into the Whirlpool in the lower river near Devil's Hole. "Whirlpool" and "Devil's Hole" are scary words to a newbie visitor.

And do you know when that fear is at its pinnacle? It's at that point in the voyage when you are so close to the Falls itself that you think you are entering the gates of Heaven (or the other place). It's at that point when all you see are sheets of falling water, and all you hear is a thundering roar. If you get any closer, you'll be climbing straight up to the Upper Niagara. The engines struggle to keep up with the awesome current. It is at that moment when your guests are most vulnerable and most dependent on you for reassurance. It is precisely then that I pull out a red rain poncho from under my blue one and slip it on so I stand out in the crowd. I place a Revolutionary War general's hat on my head. I add a long feather for effect. I attach a big name tag that reads, "Scotty - First Mate." I position myself at the tip of the bow, and stand on a small footstool I smuggled on board. I assume a pose like Washington crossing the Delaware.

I pull out my bullhorn, find the captain in the wheelhouse, look him in the eye, and exclaim, "I've giv'n her all she's got captain, an' I canna give her no more! We had better turn back now," I exclaim.

And, of course, as if the captain was actually listening to that nut in the red raincoat and peacock hat, he turns the boat around and heads for port. As I descend from my perch, and run past security, I am immediately greeted by handshakes and applause by all on deck. They all want to shake my hand and thank me for saving their lives. I am in great demand as a tour guide, and now you can be too. Just remember to use the facts you have, and make up the rest.

Men's Cologne and a Hug From My Pharmacist

I'm at that age where my local pharmacy pops up in my "recent locations" list in my car's GPS. "Two minutes to your pharmacy Bob. Traffic is light!" my phone tells me when I get into the car.

My particular pharmacy is inside a grocery store. It has its own separate entrance and you have to go through a vestibule before you get to the pharmacy counter.

It is a well-known rule in my neighborhood that shopping carts are not allowed in the vestibule. A huge sign with red letters looms over the entrance. "No Carts Allowed!" A security guard with a silver badge stands by to enforce this rule.

Sometimes on a Saturday I plant myself on the seat of the blood pressure machine outside the pharmacy entrance just to watch people with carts being turned away. It's great entertainment.

It's a big dilemma for some folks. They appear to be torn between two hard options: "I really want my blood pressure meds, but what if someone steals my English muffins!"

Experienced pharmacy visitors like me come prepared. I have a collection of RFID tracking chips tied to my handheld GPS. I surreptitiously place the chips in every item in my basket before entering the pharmacy. Once, just as I was paying for some ibuprofen, I got an alert on my device that my English muffins were traveling south in the cereal aisle! I flagged down the store police who intercepted the thief in bulk candy. He surrendered the muffins without incident.

We have three cash registers at my pharmacy counter to keep the lines moving. They keep everyone's medicine in white plastic boxes on a big shelf behind the counter. They are arranged alphabetically. Secrecy is a big deal to pharmacists. They try to be discreet when they fill your prescription. When they ask you to sign for your meds, they give you a clipboard with a slider on it that hides the name of the person who picked up his prescription before you.

I don't really get this secrecy part of the pill-dispensing business. The guy ahead of me in line was Fred Jones. The cashier won't let me see Fred's signature on the clipboard for privacy reasons. But I already know his full name and his birthday too because she had already asked him out loud and I could hear his answer. I'm probably going to send Fred a birthday card next month that will make his day. I just don't understand why I can't admire his penmanship on the clipboard.

People ask interesting questions when they pick up their meds. "Will this make me sleepy?" young adults often ask. We older folks secretly hope that our meds will make us sleepy.

Bertha is my favorite pharmacist. She has the most beautiful smile and infectious laugh. She is one of those people who is beautiful inside and out and brings joy to everyone she meets. She probably cures a lot of people with that smile and laugh. Last Thursday, she filled a prescription for me. As I was signing the clipboard she leaned toward me and asked what I was wearing.

"It's a flannel shirt from Orvis."

"No silly, I mean your cologne!"

"Oh, it's Antaeus from Chanel," I replied, "I wear it because Chef Emeril LaGasse wears it too."

I realized immediately that I had crossed a personal boundary. What you splash on your face after a shave is one thing. Why you do it is quite another!

Too much information, I thought, but it was too late. My comment was floating in the air like bubbles blown by kids, and she took it as an invitation.

Her response floored me. "Can I give you a hug?" she asked with a sparkle in her eye.

Well, I was taken aback as she jumped around the counter with her arms wide open. I looked behind me at the other customers for approval and suggestions. The little kids seemed fearful, but the ladies my age encouraged me to go for it. So there we were, smack-dab in the middle of the grocery store pharmacy in a big old friendly hug. I'm not sure if there are laws or social norms about hugging your pharmacist in public, but I was living in the moment and loving it.

The hug didn't last long. It was just a fleeting moment of goodwill between a pill dispenser and her customer. I threw my prescription bottle into my basket with the English muffins and headed for the checkout. I wondered what had just happened.

Later that evening, I looked at my pill bottle sitting on the end table, and contemplated opening it.

I didn't bother. I didn't need to. I already felt better.

I'd been hugged by my pharmacist.

My "itis"

I went to see a doctor yesterday. My wife came with me to ensure that truth be told and fiction be left at the door.

"On a scale of one to ten, how would you describe your pain?" the doctor asked.

Well, that all depends on whether you are using the Male Pain Scale or the Female Pain Scale. On my scale, it's a nine. On my wife's scale, it's a three.

I think my foot is about to fall off at the ankle. I'm wondering if I'll ever walk again.

My wife suggested a Band-Aid and an aspirin. "Once the aspirin kicks in, you can just walk it off."

Knowing this, I lied to the doctor. "It's a six," I told him.

Then comes the next question. "How did it happen?"

I'm a guy. I used to be an athlete. In my mind, I still am. There is no way I am going to answer with the truth.

I find myself perspiring as I consider the myriad lies that I am prepared to tell. I even rehearsed a few before my wife said she was coming with me.

I grimace at the mere thought of the first lie I am prepared to tell. The doctor misinterpreted my grimacing as evidence of severe pain. That's fine with me. That's what I was shooting for. The more pain the better. I'm aiming for a hospital admission as soon as possible.

Just as I am about to spin a vivid tale about climbing a mountain and falling 30 feet into a steep ravine, I remember that my wife is right there, literally at my side. I catch myself just before the prevarication leaves my lips. I am then made sharply aware of her presence when she utters a single word to the doctor.

"Treadmill!" she says, with a smug smile.

"Treadmill?" the doctor repeats.

At this point, I'm wishing I could melt away into the corner. I sensed that I was the only patient he had ever treated for a treadmill injury.

"Yes, a treadmill," my wife says before I can explain that someone had knocked me off the treadmill, that it had exploded under me during an earthquake, or that I had been walking so fast that the belt had flown off its rollers.

"He increased the speed from two and a half to three and a half miles an hour and increased the incline from zero to five percent at the same time." She pointed skyward as she described the incline.

She wasn't through. "Then he walked 8,888 steps while watching his heart rate jump into the orange zone on his iPad at the same time!" She was having entirely too good a time with her tale.

"How old are you?" the doctor asks.

I contemplated a well-crafted lie.

I could feel my wife's stare. There was no way out but to tell the truth. "I'm 62."

And then came the reprimand, out of nowhere. "You're 62 and you decided it was a good idea to walk uphill?"

Well, now I was flummoxed! A different doctor, the one who had replaced my knee, had advised me to avoid the treadmill. But I really liked the way my iPad talked to my heart rate sensor and glowed orange when I started to sweat.

I'm not usually one to share or write about personal health issues, unless it will likely result in deliveries of chicken noodle soup to my home. But, to help others, you should know this . . .

It turns out that I have an "itis." There are approximately 101 "itises" on WebMD.com. Mine is ranked 99th in importance. Some "itises" are very serious. Some just sound serious, even if they aren't. Mine isn't serious, and it doesn't even sound serious. In fact, mine is so "not serious" that doctors haven't even settled on a common spelling.

My "itis" really does sound like it can be cured with some witch hazel and a Band-Aid. I'm thinking of renaming my "itis" to attract the sympathy I fully deserve. "Profounditis." "Reallybigitis." "Painfulitis." These are all possibilities.

But my "itis" can't be cured with witch hazel. I tried. Witch hazel really stings. Telling my sister-in-law about it stings more. She suffers from the same affliction.

I called her to compare symptoms and remedies. We talked for half an hour before we caught ourselves.

"Just listen to us," she said, "We sound just like our parents."

I had to agree. Here we were sharing our common ailments instead of discussing where we would go dancing that night. I cut the call short. I didn't want to end up like those old guys at the local coffee shop comparing medical problems over breakfast.

I did learn something from that call. I learned that my sister-in-law and I both treat our "itises" the same way. We both use cruise control to avoid applying too much pressure to the brake and accelerator pedals. Brake and accelerator pedals hurt our "itis!"

Who knew that this was an effective remedy for an "itis" that even doctors don't know how to spell? My sister-in-law uses her cruise control to get out of her driveway. I use mine to lead a parade of agitated neighbors down my street at 15 miles an hour. I don't care. They are just "agitated." I have an "itis!"

Wagging Tails and Hearts of Gold

There is nothing quite like a furry, tail-wagging, beautiful, barking, little cuddler of a best friend to warm your heart. Such was my best friend, Lovey, but it wasn't always so.

I first met this beautiful Sheltie in the summer of 1983 when my fiancée said "yes" meaning, "yes," I could meet her dog. As I approached Lovey in my future in-laws' family room, she eyed me with suspicion. She was two years old and she belonged there. I did not, and she let me know.

I slowly approached with my hand palm-down beneath her chin. I'm a dog lover and they usually know it. I let her sniff and sense and size me up before I tried to pet her.

"Rar-rar-rar-rar-rar," she grumbled as she grit her teeth. "Back off." She let me know that she was a lady and it was too soon to ask her to dance.

Our courtship continued for the next few years. I

tried everything to win her over—liver treats, tennis balls, and endless "good girls" of praise. Nothing worked. Dogs are known to be great judges of character, but this princess was so mistaken, and I had no clue why. And then it dawned on me. It was her name. Could it be? Did she really overhear me?

A month after we met, Lovey escaped from the yard. We were frantic looking for her. We split up and canvassed the neighborhood. Up and down the streets we walked, all calling her name, loudly and publicly, everybody but me. I just couldn't bring myself to call the name "Lovey" out loud, not in public anyway.

I just couldn't get Thurston Howell III from Gilligan's Island out of my head. I just couldn't bring myself to call out-loud the name of a millionaire's wife on a deserted desert isle. As I searched, I could only muster, "Here Sheltie dog! Please come home!" while I muttered under my breath, "Who would give a dog a name like Lovey?"

I paid a heavy price for my chauvinistic silliness. First, Ellen asked why I wouldn't call Lovey by name in the search. She made me so nervous twisting her engagement ring halfway off her finger that I didn't notice Lovey's ears perk up.

I tried to explain that it was such a silly name that no guy would say it out loud on the street. Ellen wasn't a fan of Gilligan's Island and cocked one eyebrow perplexedly when I told her that The Professor was one of my heroes. Lovey showed me her teeth and stared me down even worse than before. I was headed for the dog pound for sure.

It took many months for me to win Lovey's trust after that incident. Only "adventure" rides with her in my blue 1989 GMC Safari mini-van, with a stereo AM/FM radio, and the McDonald's drive-thru window helped her to see the true me, the "I love all dogs, and even those named Lovey!"

I apologized to her often on those rides. I told her I was sorry. I told her that I loved her name, that it was beautiful. Sometimes I opened the window in the van and said her name out loud in public. "This is Lovey," I said to the McDonald's drive-thru lady. Lovey loved McDonald's hamburgers, sans the bun. It was our little secret. We don't really know what goes on inside the brains of our pets, but when I said "adventure" I'm pretty sure Lovey thought "hamburger."

Our relationship improved with every Happy Meal. Before long, she was giving me her paw, speaking when I asked, and fetching tennis balls. She would open and close doors and even open the refrigerator if I asked her to. She was one smart and loyal dog. And it only took an apology and a few hamburgers for me to learn that. But I didn't really know how smart she was until our daughter was born.

As all new parents know, we all share one thing in common, sleep deprivation. Our daughter put us to the test, every two hours for two months. But we were smart. We were college educated. We read parenting books. We had a plan. We would not be sleep deprived. We kept a notebook, a careful log of every bottle of formula she consumed, of every diaper we changed. We took turns.

Our notes were impeccable for the first ten days. "Two ounces of formula at 2 a.m.," I wrote.

"Two and a half ounces at 4 a.m.," Ellen added.

"Diaper changed at 6 a.m.," I wrote.

"Burped her at 7 a.m.," added Ellen.

This continued for days, then weeks. Then, one day, or night (I really don't remember), I noticed an odd entry in our log. It was barely legible, written by a mom, or maybe by a dad.

"I don't know if she ate, drank, or if I changed her diaper—and I don't care!"

Lovey was staying with us for the winter. And, all this time, unbeknownst to us, she watched this all take place, soaked it all in, and never uttered a bark.

We were doing an awful lot of laundry in those first few months of newborn bliss and hell. It was non-stop until our gas dryer failed. The repair guy came over quickly, but it needed a part. I think it was a $2,000 part, but maybe that was for a car muffler. It was all such a blur.

We hadn't slept in weeks. We didn't care. The repair

guy told us we could still use the dryer until the part arrived, as long as we remembered to shut off the gas valve in the basement after every load. I promised I would.

And then it happened...

Our bedroom and our daughter's bedroom were separated by the laundry room and the kitchen, where Lovey slept. It was 4 a.m. We were all sound asleep. Lovey whined. We ignored her. She cried louder. We put pillows over our ears. Then she barked.

"Please change her diapers," I asked Ellen.

"Dogs don't wear diapers," she mumbled.

I got up. I gave Lovey food and water. She ignored me. I tried to let her out the back door. She wouldn't go. I begged her to go outside. She wouldn't budge. In desperation, I turned on the light in the laundry room, inhaled deeply, and asked her loudly, "What do you want?"

It was at that moment that I smelled the gas.

Now, here's the amazing part. I looked Lovey straight in her beautiful brown eyes and simply said, "It's OK Lovey. I know what's wrong. Go to bed." She turned around and went to bed as I opened all the windows and went into the basement to turn off the gas valve. Lovey had saved our lives.

A couple of years later, her time with us was coming to a close, and it was time to say goodbye. I volunteered to take her to the vet that one last time. Ellen had known her longer but I was "strong" so I volunteered.

"We're going on an adventure, Lovey." But she wasn't interested in McDonald's.

I held her paw until the end and made it out of the vet's office feeling OK. I started my van and made it just to the street when it started to rain, but not from clouds. I opened the windows and said her beautiful name out loud. I couldn't leave the parking lot for the next 30 minutes. I couldn't see the road through the tears.

We've never been without two Shelties since the day Lovey saved our lives. Sheena helped us to cope with losing Lovey, and Missy helped us to cope with losing Sheena. Missy and Mia greet us every day with wagging tails and hearts of gold. I don't know what they are thinking, or what they are dreaming about when they sleep, but I'm pretty sure they would save our lives if need be. Maybe they already have.

Shaving Cream in the Passenger Compartment

When I was five years old, I watched my dad put whipped cream all over his face. I marveled at his self-control. He never licked it off. He scraped it off with a metal tool, wasting the fluffy part of a hot fudge sundae, slinging it into the sink, rinsing his tool under a stream from the faucet, and then going back to scrape some more.

I watched him do this every day. He mowed his face the same way every morning, in the same pattern he used on the front lawn. He scraped perfectly parallel rows of foam, one at a time, from ear to ear. He even whistled when he did it.

What a waste! He could have made a whole banana split with all that whipped cream!

Boys want to be like their dads. So when my parents weren't looking I would lather all sorts of delicious toppings on my face—Cool Whip, Reddi-Wip, and even I Can't Believe It's Not Butter! I would sneak these goodies into the bathroom, stand on a stool in front of the mirror, and try to sling the confections into the sink like my dad. But I failed miserably at this thing called shaving. I couldn't bring myself to wash the toppings down the drain.

I did this for years, until one day, when I was thirteen, my dad met me outside the bathroom door. He extended his hand and asked me for the can of Reddi-Wip. I thought he was mad but he just smiled. He took my whipped cream and handed me a can of Barbasol.

"Use this instead."

Well, of course I had to taste it first. And I spit it out like a volcano erupting.

My dad just watched me do it.

"Yuck," I said, "that stuff tastes awful!" The mystery was solved as my dad handed me a single blade Gillette razor and showed me how to use it. I had arrived. I was a man. I was shaving like my dad.

Shaving is a funny thing. At first you really look forward to it. We were artists in the 70s with mutton chops, sideburns, and handlebars. By my late 20s the mutton chops were gone, but the moustache remained. My fiancée loved it and told me so. I learned how much she loved it one day in 1982. She was singing in a musical in Buffalo, and I was working at a desk in Cincinnati.

I decided to surprise her at the Friday evening performance. I drove all day to make that date, and stopped to shave at a highway rest stop. The mirror was foggy and

I took too much off the left side of my moustache, then too much off the right, and so on. Before I knew it, my upper lip was bare-naked. I lost my identity in a rest stop on the New York State Thruway that day. But, no matter, my love was singing in *Annie*, and I had brought her a bouquet of roses all the way from Cincinnati.

It is not really possible to describe the changing look on my fiancée's face as she moved from utter delight knowing that I would drive 500 miles to hear her sing to complete disdain when she saw that I had completely removed my sixteen-year-old moustache on the road to the theater. It was like watching a thunderbolt strike from a fluffy cloud on a mostly sunny day. I grew that moustache back as soon as I could, and haven't been without it since. I meticulously shave and groom that moustache every day. Such is true love.

A few days ago, I bought a can of EDGE® shaving cream. I've been shaving with EDGE® my entire adult life. I love this stuff. The can fell from the shopping bag onto the seat when I stopped at a stop sign. Then, at a traffic light, I didn't notice when it fell to the floor. When I took a left turn for home, the can rolled under the front passenger seat and became perfectly aligned in the track under the seat, where it found a new home.

My wife drove us to a restaurant later that evening. I gently moved the power passenger seat rearward to let my knees breathe. I didn't notice the sound of the shaving cream cap as it popped off and headed for the rear compartment. My satellite radio drowned out the gentle hissing sound as my power seat depressed the lever. A pleasant fragrance of menthol filled the compartment. I wondered which cologne I splashed on my face that day as my wife gave me a loving glance.

As I opened the door in the restaurant parking lot, I knew for sure that this was going to be one of those special marital moments that we will always remember. I stood next to the door as green layers of shaving gel oozed from the passenger compartment and onto my shoes. The gel turned into white foam on contact. I looked to my wife for help. She looked perplexed. The EDGE® gel was out of her field of view. So I reached my hand under the seat and pulled out a big green blob to show her.

"What's that?" she asked.

"I think it's shaving cream."

I was looking for sympathy and a paper towel. What I got was hysterical laughter. I love my wife, but she is utterly useless in a shaving cream emergency situation like this.

"What should I do?"

"Keep scooping!"

And so I did, for fifteen minutes. Scoop after scoop after scoop. That stuff smells great, is sticky, and never-ending.

I thought of my dad as I scooped that cream out of my car, just like he scooped it into the sink when I was a kid.

A crowd gathered to watch the events unfold. A television news crew arrived just as I finished the evacuation. A lot of people don't know this, but you can fill an entire handicap parking spot with the contents of just one can of EDGE® shaving cream. I know this from experience.

I took my car to the car wash the next day for a professional detailing. It was still leaking and foaming when the attendant opened the passenger side door.

"Shaving cream?" he asked.

"Yep!"

"Sensitive skin in the orange can?" he asked.

"No, aloe gel in the green can."

He nodded knowingly with the confidence of a car wash guy who had seen this before. He pointed to a shelf full of shaving cream cans of every famous brand.

"Wife laughed at you?"

"Uh-huh!" I said, "and it's sticky."

He knew all about it, and we bonded over coffee as he told me not to worry.

I am undaunted. I love my wife. Tomorrow morning I will shave again!

Punctuation and Emoticons

I've long enjoyed an intimate relationship with punctuation marks. They really do all the work in the English language and get so little of the credit—sort of like offensive linemen on a football team.

I mastered them with pride early in life. I surprised my kindergarten teacher on show-and-tell day by bringing in a shoebox full of punctuation marks I had collected in my Pre-K years. Even she didn't know that there were fourteen different types of marks until I pulled them out of the box one by one, calling each by name and explaining their function.

I don't think she was all that impressed. When I got to "ellipsis," only number eight on my list, she stopped my presentation and asked me to take a note to the principal. I have always suspected that it was a suggestion from my teacher that I be referred to the school psychologist for evaluation.

Most college and graduate students probably can't name all the different types of marks. These marks can be confusing. For example, many adults and most children don't know the difference between a hyphen and a dash, let alone that there are two types of dashes—an "en" dash and an "em" dash. A dash is also the name of a running race and the name of a small grocery store in my hometown.

Probably most people know what a period is and what it is used for, and that it shouldn't be confused with a dot atop an "i," but I suspect that most folks don't really know why writers sometimes string together three or four periods in a row and call it an ellipsis (not to be confused with an ellipse, which is a curve in a plane surrounding two focal points such that the sum of the distances to the two focal points is constant for every point on the curve, which explains why most people study liberal arts instead of mathematics.)

But I digress. I am an amateur writer now, so I will tell you the truth. When a writer wants to express a thought, and then starts meandering through his vocabulary and dictionary looking for words and gets so lost that he forgets why he opened the refrigerator door in the first place, and then starts wondering where he left his car keys, and then suddenly remembers he was writing a sentence, well . . .

It is very embarrassing for a writer to forget what he wanted to write, so to avoid this red-faced emotion you just type three periods in a row and leave your reader in suspense and make it all look planned. Every skilled writer knows that when a reader comes upon an ellipsis that she will automatically finish the sentence, and the thought, in her own mind, and she will finish it better than you ever could have written it yourself, and yet will still give you the credit. It's a beautiful thing.

Some punctuation marks got me into trouble in my school days. I will forever be scarred by a teacher-student encounter with parentheses. I always liked the way left and right parentheses looked standing next to each other side by side. Like brother and sister or husband and wife, they just looked so happy close to one another that I could never bring myself to fill the space between them with words. Sometimes, though, I would tip them sideways on the page, draw little legs on the one on the bottom, add a head and tail and a leash. I loved making Dachshunds out of parentheses turned sideways, but my teachers always sent me to the cloakroom when I did this.

I can't help but feel sorry for the semi-colon. It's not a whole colon after all. I don't even know how much of a colon a semi-colon is, but whoever named it had no confidence that it could do the same great job that a colon could do. What does "semi" mean anyway? I think it means "part of." So, it's natural for a kid to think he should use it in part of a whole sentence, but that won't help you on the AP English exam.

I've ranked my fourteen punctuation marks in order

of how much I like them. I did this secretly in my head one evening while my wife and I were watching a Hallmark Channel Christmas movie. By the time the single woman with a great job as an investment banker in a big city came to Pleasant Valley where no one worked and everyone baked cookies and cupcakes, met the single guy she used to date in high school, won over the heart of his young child, fell in love and opened a bakery, I had decided that my all-time favorite punctuation mark in the whole English language is—drum roll—the exclamation point!

I think this is my favorite punctuation mark because it always makes me feel good when I read it or write it! Life is short, and most English sentences are dry, dull, boring, and uninteresting. Oh sure, you can try and spice up a sentence with exciting words or funny phrases, but nothing fills your heart with optimism and hope quite like an exclamation point.

It's so special that it's the only one of the fourteen marks with two different names. One of the great mysteries of the English language is why this two-part vertical expression of excitement is both an exclamation mark and an exclamation point.

My colleagues in the law have often criticized me for excessive use of the exclamation point in my everyday correspondence, but I've never met a sentence that couldn't be improved by one. It's even better than italics, bolding, or underlining. And I know that some of my friends share my enthusiasm. I won't name names, but sometimes when I post a story on Facebook, these friends leave a nice comment with sweet, kind words, capped off by not one, not two, but sometimes even three or more exclamation points!!!! I can assure you that this expression of love is not taught in English class, or condoned by English teachers, but it should be.

When I see a plurality of exclamation points, lined up side by side, marching across the page like Shriners in a parade, it just makes me feel good. It feels like a non-stop barrage of pats on the back or air-kisses being blown my way. I try to send them as much as I receive them.

Personally, I think three exclamation points standing side by side trumps one "thumbs-up" emoticon every time. Speaking of which, I am deep in study and very confused about these supposed representations of my emotion. I haven't come close to understanding them, and I fear they may be dangerous if misused.

I can barely make them out on my phone without a magnifying glass. They started innocently enough as a colon and half of a parentheses to resemble a smiley face, but oh how they've grown. At last count my phone had 756 emoticons that were at my disposal. I've never really felt like a skyscraper or a banana. I have no clue how to feel like a cactus (prickly I guess), nor do I know how to feel like a zucchini, but there they are on my phone. I don't even recognize 97 of the emoticons in my library. I have no idea what they are or when I should use them.

I worry that I am bereft of many important emotions. Sometimes I feel like Mr. Spock on Star Trek. I don't really know the difference between a smiley face with no teeth and a smiley face with teeth. When should you use one instead of the other?

I've recently enrolled in an Emoticon 101 course at an online university so I can make more intelligent emoticon decisions.

Of course, the least understood emoticon on Facebook is the red heart. First, the name of someone you used to date in junior high appears as someone you should be friends with. Day after day, you see this name and this profile photo. You hear Mark Zuckerberg whispering in your ear. "Go ahead, click it, send the request." Your name and profile are coming up in her newsfeed too, because Mark gets his jollies this way.

You think to yourself: She's married now, and so am I, so it's probably OK. Then you think about it for weeks. You pray about it. Then you ask your wife if it is OK if you send a friend request to a girl you walked home from school in seventh grade.

This is when my wife gives me that, "You really ponder strange things and that's why I love you" look, before she tells me to go for it.

And then it happens . . .

One of your friends, maybe a total stranger you befriended yesterday, but maybe someone you had a crush on in junior high, posts something you love, or leaves you a sweet comment, or makes you smile, or makes you laugh, or touches your heart, or makes your day.

You want to respond but you have only six options—a blue "like," a red heart, a "ha-ha" face, a "wow" face, a teary sad face, or a disapproving road-rage face (which I would never use and immediately unfriend anyone who does.) You can only pick one. And, like the Sicilian in The *Princess Bride*, you must choose wisely. You ponder your options. You wonder. If I click the heart, am I sending a message that I love the comment, love the person, or both? Will my heart be misconstrued?

All you need is love. Go ahead, make someone's day! Click the heart!! And then add a few exclamation marks!!!

Top of the World

I admit it. It was all my idea. But I never thought any of our moms, least of all mine, would actually say yes.

The eight of us—Louie, Marv, Dan, Ron, Mike, Jim, Tony, and me, all high school juniors and great friends—were in this together from the start. It was all for one and one for all. If any mom or dad said no, we were going to call the whole thing off.

I had to sell my seven friends on selling this adventure to their parents.

We had our planning meeting in Mike's backyard because he had a swimming pool. My seven friends stood in the water, and I stood on the deck with an easel and a map.

"Gentlemen," I said, "we will lubricate our chains, buy spare inner tubes, put new tires on our bikes, load as much food as we can carry, and depart from our houses at 4 a.m. on July 1. We'll meet in front of Gaskill Junior High at 4:15 a.m."

My seven colleagues listened silently.

I pointed to the map. "We will take Hyde Park Boulevard south to Buffalo Avenue. We'll turn left, cross the Grand Island Bridge, and take Grand Island Boulevard across the island. We'll take Niagara Street to Clinton and go east to Bailey Avenue. We'll ride Route 62 all the way to Hamburg, then go east on Route 391 to the 219. We'll ride the 219 south to Cotter Road in Ellicottville, where we'll camp overnight at my Uncle Ernie's cabin.

"The next day we ride to Allegany State Park. We stay a week in Allegany, then we ride to Short Tract where Jim has a trailer. We stay overnight and the next day we ride to Letchworth State Park. We stay a week at Letchworth, and then ride back to Niagara Falls. Any questions?"

"Just one," said Jim. "Why do we have to leave at 4 a.m.?"

"All epic adventures start at 4 a.m.," I said. "And we have to get to my uncle's cabin before 7 p.m. because my mom won't let me ride my bike after dark."

That's right, we were planning a 250 mile bicycle trip across the highways and back roads of Western New York and I was worried about my mom finding out we were riding after dark.

"Why do we want to do this?" Marv asked, with an emphasis on "why."

Marv was our class president, quarterback of our football team, and all the girls loved him, so I knew how to entice him.

"Because I heard a rumor that Zeta Phi Delta sorority is going to be camping in Allegany that whole week."

Marv broke into a knowing grin at this news. Tony smiled. Louie and Mike nodded in approval. There were grins all around.

"So where will we sleep?" Louie asked.

Louie was a fisherman and outdoorsman. He brought his fly fishing rod to show-and-tell in kindergarten, so of course he would ask about the essentials.

"We can camp on my Uncle Ernie's front lawn the first night," I said. "Sleeping bags and tube tents."

"So what is this going to cost us?" Ron asked, in between cannonballs.

Ron knew from an early age that he was going to be an accountant. Even back then he knew all about debits and credits.

"You all have to give me six bucks towards the cabin rental at Red House Lake."

"But that's three weeks of my allowance," Jim lamented.

"How much is it worth for you to sit by a campfire with the Zeta Phi girls with no parents around for a hundred miles?"

Jim's expression changed as he calculated how many of his baseball cards he'd have to sell to join us on this trip.

"When we get to Letchworth, we'll rent a campsite that will cost us two dollars per night." I made the next point very clear. "My friends, no one comes on this trip without a whole twenty dollars in his pocket." I knew that was a lot of money, but we would need at least $160. We could live like kings for two whole weeks with that kind of dough.

"What's a tube tent?" Jim asked.

"It's like a big plastic trash bag, except it's orange and six feet long with a hole at each end," Danny said. He was a Boy Scout. He knew everything there was to know about camping.

"What we will we eat?" Tony asked.

"Beans. And more beans. And maybe some fish from Red House Lake if Louie shows us how to catch them. Maybe we'll find some fruit stands along the road. And everybody had better bring a canteen full of water."

"What about the beer?' Louie asked.

"Guys, may I remind you that Danny and I have been buying Molson Golden from the delicatessen at 22nd and Grand since we were fourteen. Remember, I have a moustache and fake ID from Nevada. Beer will not be a problem."

Even the skeptical were now onboard.

And then they stumped me with the big question: "How do we ask our parents?"

"Gentlemen, you are all on your own with respect to parental permission."

This was our big concern. How were we ever going to

convince all of our parents to let us go?

Jim was the only one who wasn't worried. He had seven brothers and sisters. He could have walked to Allegany State Park, stayed a week, and walked back home, and his parents wouldn't have even missed him.

Miracle of miracles, one by one, our parents all said yes. And there was very little discussion about it.

"My mom said I'm going to get hemorrhoids from riding a bike that far!" Tony told me later. I'm pretty sure Tony didn't know what a hemorrhoid was, and I wasn't too sure myself, except that I had seen a Preparation H commercial on TV so I reassured him there was a cure.

One of the great mysteries of our young lives up to that point was how our parents could so quickly give us permission to leave our homes for two weeks in the summer to ride our bikes hundreds of miles across Western New York.

We openly wondered if they had stopped loving us. It was only much later in life, when we had teenagers of our own, that we realized our parents probably would have let us ride all the way to California.

Seven of us arrived at Gaskill at 4:15 a.m. Jim was late. Jim was always late. But he was our friend, so we waited for him.

We had a variety of 10-speed bicycles. Louie and I had bright yellow Schwinn Super Sports. They were heavy but they were solid. Mike had a Gitane. "Gitane" is French for

"Gypsy Woman" and Mike somehow thought that a Gypsy Woman bike was sexy to enough to attract the girls. Others rode Raleighs. Jim rode a Huffy. We teased that it would make him huff and puff all the way to Allegany.

I pushed the start button on my odometer at precisely 4:25 a.m. and watched the dial on my speedometer rotate clockwise as we started to pedal. Our adventure had begun.

The city was quiet as we made our way in a follow-the-leader line, heading south down Hyde Park Boulevard. There were no cars on the road at this early hour. Even the birds were still sleeping in the trees. Our bikes were laden with sleeping bags, tube tents, and cans of beans in front panniers, rear panniers, and handlebar bags. We all had horns, bells, and headlights, and a frame mounted air pump just in case.

We all wore Converse sneakers, white tube socks calf-high with colored rings around the tops, shorts, and T-shirts. Our windbreakers flapped in the cool morning breeze. I wore a pink towel around my neck. I don't know why I did that, but it brought me comfort. To this day, I am seldom without a scarf.

As we headed down Buffalo Avenue we could see the North Grand Island Bridge in the distance as the sun rose over the upper Niagara. Lake Erie's water was rushing to the great Niagara Falls, in a big hurry to reach Lake Ontario. We could hear the roar of the Falls a couple of miles behind us. The fast-moving water reflected the morning sunlight in a thousand sparkling waves, like diamonds twinkling in the night sky. It was all so inspiring that we just started to pedal as fast as we could.

In those days, you could walk and even ride your bike over the Grand Island Bridge. They don't let you do that anymore. I suspect they closed the sidewalks because some poor kid on a bike went over the railing. And that could happen. I clocked 40 miles an hour on my speedometer on our way down the arch, and I wasn't even pedaling. I remember thinking that just one small pebble could cause a major wipeout—maybe even toss us into the river.

We had only gone a mile when Ron yelled, "Flat!" That was our agreed-upon alert word when someone blew a tire. Ron was second in line behind me when it happened.

Just like school bus drivers leaving the parking lot in the morning, we riders veered alternatingly to the right and to the left to avoid rear-ending Ron. Louie and Dan jumped off their bikes and ran to help. Three guys fixed that tire in ten minutes flat and we were on our way again.

You learn a lot about your friends on a long bike ride, like how fast they will come to your aid when you are in trouble. You also learn that they might not like the music you play on your transistor radio. I was the only one with a radio, but I thought all my friends should listen to it as we rode. Turns out I was the only fan of WBNY 96.1 Easy Listening.

"Turn it off!" Louie demanded.

"Any station that doesn't play the Allman Brothers isn't worth listening to," Marv added.

We rode south down Niagara Street and reached Niagara Square in downtown Buffalo around 6 a.m. The morning Courier-Express had already been delivered to the houses we passed. One old man in a robe was picking up his paper at the end of his driveway as the eight of us rode by. You should have seen his face as he seemed to wonder where we were going and where we had come from.

If you've ever ridden on a bicycle for an extended distance, you know the thoughts that enter your mind along the journey, especially if you are riding with a group. Your neck gets sore first, and then your arms, and then that part of your body in contact with your seat. Ironically, your legs are the last to tire. But if you are seventeen and riding with your friends, you keep all these aches and pains to yourself, and just try to keep up. Eventually, you ride on adrenaline alone. No one wants to be the first to ask for a break, but everybody wants one.

I knew about these feelings because I had ridden my bike to Ellicottville the summer before. I had some experience in this regard, so I had planned a lunch break for an hour in Hamburg. It's good to have a preplanned rest stop. As we sat on a curb in front of a Your Host restaurant, we munched on peanut butter and jelly sandwiches our moms had packed. We lacked the funds for a hamburger in Hamburg.

The hardest stretch of riding was on the old 219 between North Boston and Ellicottville. If you are in a car, you might not even notice the hills. But to us, they were mountains. Our 30-pound bikes were loaded with 50 pounds of gear. We had to use first gear for every steep climb. That's the gear where you are pedaling so fast and furious and seemingly going nowhere. You just think you are never going to get to the top of the hill. And there were so many of them!

I don't know how many mountains there are exactly on the old 219, but when you are a teenager on a bike, it seems like a thousand. Eventually, we splintered into small groups. I led the first group of three with Ron and Dan. Marv led the second group with Louie, Tony, and Mike. Jim was an island onto himself. Jim was a decent athlete, but he was the youngest, and he had to ride the Huffy.

We only had one scare on this leg of the trip. Seven of us stopped at a fruit stand at the top of a really high mountain. The locals called it Nunweiler Hill, but we called it Everest. We had each devoured a handful of juicy homegrown peaches. "Hey, where's Jim?" Louie asked.

Marv broke out the binoculars.

"He was behind me the last time I checked," Mike said.

"Well, when did you last check?" asked Marv as he scanned the horizon.

"Don't know. Maybe an hour ago," Mike replied between bites.

We waited and worried, and then we waited and worried some more, except for Tony, who was pretty absorbed reading the directions on the side of a Preparation H tube. We were about to look for a way to call the police.

"Hold on. Is that him?" Louie shouted.

Well, at first he was only a speck in Marv's binoculars at the base of the mountain, but Jim's sweating, panting face got larger and larger as he climbed. He was standing over his saddle and swinging the frame from side to side with each push of the pedals. We yelled and applauded to encourage him toward the peak.

When he got to the top, he was clearly beat. "How long were you guys waiting for me?" he gasped.

"Oh, just a few minutes, Jim," Mike told him.

Such is true friendship.

The best part about climbing a hill on your bike, of course, is that eventually you get to fly down the other side. Next to jumping out of an airplane and having the parachute open, riding a bicycle down a mountain at 50 miles an hour on a hot summer day, with the wind blowing through your hair, is probably the next best feeling in the world. Not one of us touched our caliper brakes on the descent. We had worked too hard on the climb to be denied the thrill of the downhill.

Eventually gravity loses its effect and you stop gliding and start pedaling again. This is when riding a bike becomes magical. You notice everything—the serenade of the birds and crickets and the fragrance of wildflowers and fresh-cut hay. The rabbits and ground hogs stand on their hind legs to greet you, and the cows seem to nod as you pass them by. It makes you feel sorry for the people who whiz by in their cars.

We arrived at my Uncle Ernie's cabin just as the sun was setting over our shoulders. As we pedaled toward Irish Hill, we kicked up a load of dust from the dirt road. We didn't say a word to one another. We didn't need to and couldn't if we tried. Our throats were parched but our spirits were high. My uncle's old hound, Lady, galloped down the road to meet us and guide us to her home.

We all stood in line in my uncle's kitchen to use his phone to call our moms to let them know we were safe. My Aunt Annie gave each of us a tall glass of lemonade while we waited our turn. We set up our tube tents and sleeping bags on the front lawn and prayed that it wouldn't rain.

We lined up our cans of beans for dinner. They were already cooked in the can from the summer heat. We took a dip in my uncle's pool to cool off. To our great surprise, we were lured from the pool by the aroma of hamburgers cooking on the grill. I loved my Uncle Ernie.

Sleep comes easy after an 80-mile bike ride, but you dream that you are still pedaling all night long.

The next day we took the short trip to Allegany and set up camp in our paid-for cabin at Red House Lake. We were pioneers. We had shelter. We had water. We needed food. We spent the whole day fishing in rowboats in the lake.

None of us really knew how to fish except Louie, and he showed the rest of us. We caught eight perch and sixteen sunfish among the eight of us. Louie and Dan cleaned them and Mike and Marv fried them in a pan. It's a funny thing about fish memories—the sunfish we caught in the lake that day when I was seventeen became giant tuna in my dreams when I was 62.

We were all alone the first couple of days at Allegany. We spent July 4th enjoying our fresh fish dinner and watching fireflies over the lake. We talked about our future plans. Louie was going to be a nature photographer and Ron a Certified Public Accountant. Danny and Mike were planning on dental school, and I was going to be an engineer. Tony and Marv were both going to pharmacy school. Jim was still undecided and exploring his options. We didn't know what our futures would hold, but we all knew we would be friends forever.

Before long, Marv asked a pointed question. "Where are the sorority girls?"

Jim had a sister who knew a girl in the sorority, so we gave him a bunch of dimes and pointed him to a phone booth. He came back disheartened. The good news was that the girls were in Allegany State Park. The bad news was that they were seven miles away from us at Quaker Lake.

What to do? No one wanted to risk riding that far only to find out that the girls weren't there, or that there was no place for us to sleep. We were hoping we could negotiate with them to rent one of their cabins for a few days.

I felt obligated to make the trip—fourteen miles round-trip—just to find out if they had a room to let. My best friend Dan wouldn't let me go alone. Without hesitation, he picked up his bike and followed me out the door.

It wasn't just seven miles from Red House to Quaker—it was three and a half miles straight up, and three and a half miles straight down. Unlike my other friends, Danny didn't mind my transistor radio music. We listened to 1973 hits during our long ascent up Allegany Mountain, (that's what we called it.) We were in first gear the whole way up. It was agonizing. We rested for a minute when we got to the top.

And then it happened . . .

We were standing on the top of the world. We knew it. We felt it. We weren't just at the top of a mountain; we were at the beginning of our lives. We were young.

We were strong. We were invincible. And somehow, right then, Karen Carpenter decided to remind us that we were

on top of the world, looking down on creation.

She sang with that beautiful angelic voice, touching our hearts with four verses through six transistors. We both knew it was a love song. We weren't lovers, just best friends, coming of age on our bicycles. We were literally at the top of the mountain when Karen's voice came through from a distant AM radio station.

Well, Dan and I shared a good laugh at the love song

lyrics and the coincidence of our being on top of the mountain as she sang about being on top of the world. We didn't rest long. We pushed off and peddled our hearts out. The Zeta Phi girls were waiting for us after all. As we picked up speed, I heard Karen sing something about happiness and Heaven, but her words faded as we started our descent.

The signal faded completely on the other side of the mountain. We coasted downhill for three and a half miles at fifty miles an hour. It felt like we were flying. The wind was at our back and our whole lives were in front of us.

We found the sorority girls and debated ever riding back to Red House to tell our friends. Eventually we did, and we all spent the rest of the week crammed into a small cabin at Quaker Lake.

We are gentlemen. We don't kiss and tell. But hands were held, kisses shared, love affairs started, and lifelong friendships formed during that magical week at Allegany.

What happens in Allegany stays in Allegany, but Marv, Tony, and Mike went home with the sorority sisters. The remaining five of us trekked on to Letchworth.

Ron survived a near-miss with a pickup truck at the Park Road/Wolf Creek hairpin curve. He missed the truck but blew out a couple of tires and bent both rims. We lacked the funds for repair so he finished the ride home in his dad's truck. Jim had seen enough and went home with Ron and his dad.

We were down to three. Louie, Dan, and I camped at Letchworth for a few days, but we missed our friends and soon headed for home. We were the only ones to complete the full ride all the way back to Niagara Falls.

We reminisced about that trip for years.

"That was the best time ever," Dan would always say with a twinkle in his eye whenever we got together. "The best time ever!"

"Top of the world!" I'd reply. And then we would clink our glasses of Molson Golden.

I think about Dan often, especially when I hear that song. He never got the chance to become a dentist.

His signal may have faded, but I know he is riding down the other side of the mountain now, flying along with the wind blowing through his hair.

I still ride my bike every Sunday in the summer. I don't climb hills much anymore, except in my dreams. But I still look to the sky when I ride and remember those beautiful summer days of long ago. In retrospect, I did love my best friend and all my friends. That's why I'm on top of the world.

A Kid Brother's Tale... Mining for Gold on Niagara Avenue

By Michael J. Simpson

Most of the stories in this book are true, and the rest are mostly true. In this regard, I agree with Mark Twain that, "Truth is the most valuable thing we have. Let us economize it." It is difficult to discern the truth from a single perspective, especially the perspective of a storyteller. To help the reader decide fact from fiction, I leave you with this final tale from my very talented younger brother, Michael J. Simpson. A poet, teacher, and storyteller in his own right, it is my honor to give him the final word.

It was a time before YouTube, the Internet, and the Information Age. We had a yellow-paged dictionary, a set of well-thumbed encyclopedias, and a building full of books called a library.

If I had a question about something, I would ask my

mother and, more times than not, she would refer me to the dictionary or encyclopedia.

"You should be able to learn to solve your own problems," she used to say.

I was sure that she knew more than the dictionary and the encyclopedia combined. Occasionally, she would demonstrate her expansive knowledge, like every day at lunch.

One day I came home from Hyde Park School for tomato soup and a grilled cheese sandwich. I was mostly focused on my lunch and wondering if I would get to watch the Flintstones at 12:30 p.m. Mom and my older brother, Bob, were in their daily competition with the contestants on Jeopardy. I would occasionally tune in to an answer and formulate the question in my head, only to hear my mother shout the "question" before I had a chance to breathe in. It didn't help that I had to remember that Jeopardy was backwards.

My mother's title as the Queen of Knowledge was solidified for me one warm summer morning in my sixth year. I had watched a western movie the night before and learned that gold comes from digging a big hole in the earth. That was enough information to get me started on my first get rich quick scheme.

I barely slept. I was going to be a rich kid the very next day. I thought through every last detail, all three of them. I would need a shovel, a place to dig, and a partner

I could trust.

The right partner required the most thought. I weighed my options. Maybe Dougie? No. He was too young. What about my brother? No. He would try to take over. Dad perhaps? No. He'd be at work.

I soon realized that my mother was the only logical choice. Not only did I trust my mom, but I was pretty sure I needed her permission to dig a gold mine in our backyard.

I awoke early to join my mother at breakfast. Mom was at the kitchen table and it looked like she was on her second cup of coffee. She was getting ready to clean what looked to me to be an already clean house.

"Mom, I have an idea," I said.

"Oh, you do?"

I told her my plan. In retrospect, I'm pretty sure my mom considered me a great source of entertainment. She did a remarkable job of holding back her laughter. She was never dismissive. She seemed to be taking me very seriously. She gave me permission to dig in the yard.

We sealed the deal and I headed outside poor but determined not to come back until I had struck it rich.

The ground was still soft from the morning dew. I found my spot and started to dig. I filled a pail with water so I could rinse the dirt and reveal all the gold nuggets I was going to find. I was about 15 minutes into my new enterprise when I started to get discouraged. I was close to dropping from exhaustion. I had dug at least five or six shovels out of my new mine.

I sat on the ground next to the bucket. I decided it was time to start cleaning the dirt. That was just as important as digging it. It was also a lot easier.

As I reached down into the muddy water to feel around for gold nuggets, my mind started to wander. I was thinking that if the gold mine didn't work out that maybe I could turn the hole into a swimming pool.

As a test, I poured most of the water into the hole, only to watch it seep back into the earth. I turned to dump the rest of the water into the hole and noticed something shiny in the bucket.

What was that? There was a glint in the bucket, a sparkle!

Was it gold? I reached to the mud-coated bottom of the bucket and grasped the shiny rock. I wiped it on my shirt. This was it! I'm rich! I bet this is enough gold to buy every G.I. Joe in the Century catalog. I looked again, just to be sure. Yes, there it was. Gold!

I dashed into the house yelling. "Mom, Mom!" I shouted. "Come and look!"

I handed her my gold. She turned it over in her hands. She scratched at it with her fingernail.

"Hmmm..."

My anxiety grew. I could see she was constructing some type of lesson, and I was praying it was going to be about fiscal responsibility.

It wasn't. My mother was always very direct when she broke bad news. "Fool's gold," she said. She went on to tell me that it is actually called pyrite. "Repeat it three times," she said, "and it's yours forever." I wasn't about to forget the rock that dashed my dream of incredible wealth.

I think I surprised my mother by how well I took the bad news. What she didn't know is that I had a plan B to soften my disappointment. "I can turn my gold mine into a swimming pool."

"You have to dig down quite a ways," Mom said. "You'll have to dig until the dirt turns red. The red dirt is clay and clay is not porous. It will hold in the water. The dirt won't."

That seems like a lot of work, I thought. An awful lot of work.

It seemed natural at the time that my mother knew all about pyrite and the permeability properties of clay. It wasn't until years later that I started to wonder if she had a photographic memory. She just seemed to have a deep knowledge of everything she had ever heard or read. When I look back now, I appreciate that, while I was mining for gold on Niagara Avenue, I had found it in my mother's heart.

About the Author

Robert P. Simpson, born on Holy Thursday, 1956, is a patent attorney, electrical engineer, chess player, and storyteller from Niagara Falls, New York. He graduated from Rochester Institute of Technology in 1979, and received a law degree from State University of New York at Buffalo School of Law in 1987. He has practiced law for more than 30 years, written hundreds of patent applications, and told more than 60 Bob-Tales. He resides in Williamsville, New York with his wife, Ellen, and his Shelties, Missy and Mia. His wife encouraged (actually begged) him to start telling his stories to others.

www.ingramcontent.com/pod-product-compliance
Lightning Source LLC
Chambersburg PA
CBHW022215090526
44584CB00012BB/565